"Drawing on her own extensive research and experience, Maureen Healy wisely leads parents and caregivers into the heart of awakening and activating the innate confidence with which every child is born. This is a book that parents will read over and over again."

—**Michael Bernard Beckwith**, author of
Spiritual Liberation: Fulfilling Your Soul's Potential

"*Growing Happy Kids* gives parents what we all long for: a simple five-step plan to help nurture their children's self-confidence so they can handle whatever comes up smoothly."

—**Edward M. Hallowell, M.D.**, author of
The Childhood Roots of Adult Happiness

"Drawing on a wealth of experience and good-heartedness, Maureen Healy offers wise and practical strategies for adults who hope to guide children toward a lifetime of confidence and true happiness."

—**Sharon Salzberg**, author of *Real Happiness*

"Empowering children with the confidence and inner resilience to both endure mistakes and setbacks, as well as to skillfully master things, is what successfully raising happy and fulfilled kids is all about. Maureen Healy does just that in th' ive and wise integration of Eastern wisdom wit logical science, including her Five Buil nd Inner Strength, which is just w children to be a happier, healthier, more harmonious and beautiful place to urish in. I recommend *Growing Happy Kids* to every ested in passing insightful wisdom on to future generations."

—**Lama Surya Das**, author of *Awakening the Buddha Within*

"Maureen Healy's *Growing Happy Kids* is a wise handbook on how parents can, and must, instill confidence in their children. Culled from years of experience, this guide is both deeply intelligent and practical to the core."

—**Mark Banschick, M.D.**, author of *The Intelligent Divorce*

"Maureen Healy's *Growing Happy Kids* is filled with keen insights and easy-to-apply ideas that will help every parent reveal the best in their child."

—**John B. Waterhouse, Ph.D.**, president of Centers for Spiritual Living

"In *Growing Happy Kids*, Maureen Healy has given us rich and valuable tools to assist us in honoring and supporting our children in building their self-confidence and helping them become happier. It is a MUST read for all parents, educators, and people who care."

—**Edwene Gaines**, author of *The Four Spiritual Laws of Prosperity*

"Maureen Healy's vibrant 'can do' spirit imbues every page with a sense of joy and possibility, offering parents and other adults a clear roadmap to help them nurture positive, purposeful kids who can successfully navigate just about any challenge they ever face."

—**Kathy Eldon**, founder of Creative Visions Foundation and editor of *The Journey Is the Destination*

GROWING *happy* KIDS

GROWING
happy
KIDS

How to Foster Inner Confidence, Success, and Happiness

MAUREEN HEALY

Health Communications, Inc.
Deerfield Beach, Florida

www.hcibooks.com

Growing Happy Kids and the information contained in this book are not intended as a substitute for the advice and/or medical care of the reader's physician. The author of this book does not provide medical advice or prescribe the use of any form of treatment without the advice of a medical professional. The intent of this author is solely to provide information of a general nature to help you or your child in your quest for emotional, mental, spiritual, and physical well-being.

Library of Congress Cataloging-in-Publication Data

©2012 Maureen Dawn Healy

Healy, Maureen, 1972-
  Growing happy kids : how to foster inner confidence, success, and happiness / Maureen Healy.
      p. cm.
  Includes index.
  ISBN 978-0-7573-1612-8 (pbk.)
  ISBN 0-7573-1612-3 (pbk.)
  ISBN 978-0-7573-1613-5 (e-book)
  ISBN 0-7573-1613-1 (e-book)
  1. Success in children.   2. Confidence in children.   3. Happiness in children.
  4. Child rearing.   0I. Title.
  BF723.S77H43 2012
  649.6--dc23

                                                                    2011053344

HCI, its logos, and marks are trademarks of Health Communications, Inc.

Publisher: Health Communications, Inc.
          3201 S.W. 15th Street
          Deerfield Beach, FL 33442–8190

Cover design by Justin Rotkowitz
Interior design by Lawna Patterson Oldfield
Interior formatting by Dawn Von Strolley Grove

*May all children be free from suffering
and the causes of suffering.
May all children be happy.*

Contents

Introduction 1

part one **Confidence: Here to Stay!**

1 Inner Confidence . . . Really? 13

2 Real Parents, Real Stories 29

part two **The Confidence Connection**

3 The Five Building Blocks of Confidence 53

4 Bringing the Blocks to Life 93

5 The Connection Between Confidence and Happiness 131

part three **Inner Confidence for Every Kid**

6 Outer Confidence: Stepping-Stone to Success 157

7 Inner Confidence: Planting Stronger Seeds 181

8 The Inner Confidence Plan for Life 205

Giving Back   235

Acknowledgments   237

Resource Guide   239

Index   243

Introduction

During the winter of 2007, I buried myself under blankets and multiple layers of clothing every night, feeling invigorated even though it was so cold that I could still see my breath as I drifted off to sleep. I was living at the base of the Himalayan Mountains in northern India, and while this winter was particularly cold—and there was no heat—I felt stronger than I had in my entire life.

Sometimes in life we make a wish, and then boom—it comes true. This trip was the answer to my prayers: *What is inner strength?* I had wondered. Why do Tibetans—the primary ethnic group in that part of India—seem so strong, despite being exiled from their country? What do they know that I don't? Are their children the same way? Is it genetic? Can *I* develop this deeper level of power? Can it be created? Or am I stuck with the Healy gene of unhappiness?

My quest was both personal and professional. I was working in a clinic, counseling children to overcome obstacles—Dad's in prison, school stinks, Mom's an alcoholic, you've got a distraction problem—those sorts of obstacles. My clients weren't happy kids; they definitely weren't showing the deeper level of inner strength I saw so vividly in my Tibetan Buddhist friends' children. One day, I wondered aloud to a friend, "I would love to see how Tibetan kids are raised and compare their upbringing with Western children." Without skipping a beat, he said, "Why don't you do it?"

So I called Delta Airlines to inquire about my frequent flyer miles, and as fate would have it, I had just enough miles to go round-trip to South Asia for free! There was nothing stopping me. I booked a flight, took a hiatus from the clinic gig, asked my mother to watch my pug for three months, and allowed the universe to unfold the rest.

Amazing things happened on the way: I got invited to teach at a Tibetan kindergarten as a visiting teacher (just needed to brush up on my Tibetan); a Buddhist friend just happened to be going at the same time; I could attend a two-week program His Holiness the Dalai Lama was teaching on strength and happiness in his temple; and I found a place to stay for three U.S. dollars a night. My way was made magically clear, and it felt as if I was being set up to learn about the Tibetan's particular type of inner strength—what I came to call *inner confidence*.

One Monk and Many Monkeys

One day late that winter, I started up a mountain in Dharamsala— a mountain that often called my name for a hike after a morning full of Tibetan tots pulling my hair, playing puzzles, and mimicking my every move. On this particular day, I decided to climb it later than normal; the sun was shining, and it felt like it would shine forever.

Hiking alone gave me time to contemplate what I could learn from these Tibetan children and where I could glean more information about the root causes of confidence—and ultimately happiness. Up the mountain, I saw beautiful hills blanketed with rhododendrons and prayer flags streaming from every house. On my way toward a mountain overlook, I passed a yak, monks reciting mantras, and Tibetans practicing traditional dance for an upcoming performance. The hills were alive with ancient sounds.

Then, all of a sudden, I realized the sun was setting.

I scampered down the mountain as fast as I could. The sun was setting quickly, my water had run out, the temperature was dropping—and now, in front of me, I saw a band of monkeys. No way could I get around those beasts. A big grandfather-type monkey bared his fangs. I knew that when an animal shows his teeth, he's trying to scare you away—and I *was* scared. I just wanted to be in my bed, but my three-dollar-a-day hotel was down the mountain. So I stood in fear and froze.

Well, I thought, *I'm going to have to go back up the mountain and find some shelter somewhere. It'll be okay.*

It didn't feel okay, though. Seemingly out of nowhere, a monk appeared from the top of the mountain. He looked at me, and then at the monkeys. "They are scared," he said. "Yes, I know," I replied. "I'm scared, too." He smiled and said, "Follow me." Then Mr. Monk walked with certainty past those growling monkeys, exuding an air of confidence.

The monkeys backed down, letting Mr. Monk pass easily. Amazed, I followed him. The monkeys had picked up on my fear, but Mr. Monk's calmness, poise, and inner power parted that band of beasts as though they were the Red Sea. I thanked him profusely, and he evaporated into the night.

Right then, I vowed to discover what that monk knew. How could he display such peace? He only held a *mala*—Buddhist rosary beads—so whatever his secret, I knew it had to be something internal.

✳   ✳   ✳

Chances are you picked up this book for the same reasons that I traveled to be with Tibetan refugees. You want to feel strong from the inside out, without any proverbial monkeys on your back that limit your life—and you want to raise your children to experience their inner power and strength from the start, instead of constantly battling their fears and feeling frozen in their footsteps.

Arming your children with this type of inner confidence will enable them to pursue their happiest lives, make choices from a place of power, and create whatever their hearts desire. Every parent wants his or her child to be happy and to live his or her best life. As you'll soon discover, this is only possible with the creation of inner confidence.

My Inner Journey

This book was born out of my own need to feel more confident—the type of confidence that isn't easily broken or scared away by a band of equally frightened monkeys. Seeking self-confidence isn't a new search for me. It began in the seventies and eighties; I was a child of parents with problems. I don't blame them for their challenges, but for them, "good parenting" meant putting food on the table and a roof over our heads. That's okay, but it didn't help a sensitive kid learn how to feel good about herself and her capabilities.

For years, I sought confidence in external circumstances—from gold stars, pay raises, and new boyfriends to snazzy cars. That never works, though. At some point, the car breaks, the boyfriend leaves, and the job ends. In our country, the search for confidence in things is also a very common way of pursuing strength. Our culture doesn't shy away from trying to sell you something that guarantees it will make you feel better.

I also spent a significant amount of time attending workshops, reading books, and seeking mentors who would somehow lift this sense of unworthiness, insecurity, and doubt from the essence of my being. Each moved me in the right direction, but none really solved this situation—until I had the great fortune of connecting with some Buddhist teachers who guided me to my potential and connected me to the truth of inner confidence.

All of this was happening as I counseled children and adults (parents, grandparents, stepparents, foster parents, and others involved in raising children) in a variety of settings, from educational to clinical. In my work life, one question kept reappearing: How could I help this parent, teacher, or child find his or her inner strength to overcome a current challenge and, ultimately, create a happier life? This nagged at me. Even though I had an extensive background in child psychology, multiple degrees, and decades of experience, I still grappled with this question.

There seemed to be a lack of systematic approaches to cultivating this inner strength, and a lack of clarity about how to generate it in our children. More than anyone, these young people need to feel confident from the get-go so they can make choices that empower their dreams and help them be who they came here to be.

My questions persisted, and connecting with Buddhism helped me see solutions. Before I knew it, I was creating and teaching children's Buddhist-based programs around the United States and bringing those ideas abroad in more universal terms.

My organization, Growing Happy Kids, emerged from this experience. We're dedicated to planting the seeds of happiness in kids around the world. This type of enduring happiness isn't just "pie in the sky" anymore; through tapping and sharing the wisdom of the world, it has become more accessible and possible for kids, no matter where they live.

The Study of Inner Confidence

During my time in Asia, I promised myself that I would get to the bottom of what confidence really is and how I can help others develop it—specifically, how I could help parents spark it in their children.

Over the next few years, I pored through tons of clinical data and spoke with countless experts about confidence and self-esteem. Stacks of dense data fill my office. Through translators, I conducted interviews in English, Spanish, German, French, and Tibetan. My goal was to leave no stone unturned.

After many more years of private practice with kids and parents along with studying inner confidence across different disciplines, I discovered that inner confidence manifests as a result of five building blocks. In this book, I share these "Five Building Blocks of Confidence," so raising confident kids is no longer an elusive topic but something real and possible for every parent—no matter his or her situation.

Confidence Across Cultures

Cultivating confidence cuts across all cultures, and the book in your hands is a result of my international path. I have been fortunate to travel to South Asia, the banks of London, the mountains of Mexico, and across cities in the United States speaking with parents, teaching classes, and working directly with children.

Throughout this book, you'll find stories from real parents and real kids that help you not only conceptually learn about inner confidence, but "get it" on a practical level. All of my clients' names have been changed along with many other names mentioned. (Once in a while, I've kept someone's name so you can better relate to their story, like with Anne Goddard and her amazing son, Colin Goddard.)

One thing that also emerged clearly after interviewing hundreds of parents and kids: The path towards cultivating this deeper sense of strength isn't as mysterious as many of us might think. It simply results from doing things in a certain way—and that way is made clear in the Building Blocks and throughout this book. The development of inner confidence is also a prerequisite for so many positive experiences that it is essential for you to understand what it is and how to bring it to life through the Building Blocks.

What You'll Find in This Book

Growing Happy Kids is divided into three sections. In Part One, we'll define and understand the different types of confidence. I'll share the concept of outer and inner confidence along with the stages of confidence, especially as they relate to children. You'll read real-life stories to solidify your new understanding of confidence as a parent, and spend a little time in honest self-reflection. The definition of inner confidence— a deeper and more lasting type of inner strength—will become perfectly clear. And you'll hear from parents around the planet who are nurturing this deeper type of lasting strength.

Part Two of this book further develops these concepts. You'll learn about:

- **The Five Building Blocks of Confidence**—A new model to understand and develop confidence in children. The Blocks are: Biology, Beliefs, Emotions, Social, and Spiritual.
- **Implementing the Blocks**—Each Block is explained in a down-to-earth format and includes practical ideas to implement each one.

• **The Confidence-Happiness Connection**—Inner confidence
is a prerequisite for lasting happiness.

Each of these chapters offers new ideas, real-life stories, and suggestions to make your busy parenting life easier. The goal isn't to give
you more to do, but to make your time with your child as effective as
possible. If you want to raise a child to be confident from the inside
out, this book will help you accomplish that goal.

It's one of the most worthy goals any parent can hope to achieve.
An inwardly confident child can:

• Persevere and progress in the face of problems
• Become self-reliant
• Trust himself or herself
• Become a role model of real strength
• Follow his or her dreams
• Fulfill his or her potential
• Develop a deep and abiding sense of happiness

Today, we want our children to become strong from the inside
out and lead their happiest lives. This all begins with the creation of
inner confidence.

In Part Three, we'll explore what to do when confidence breaks
and how outer confidence alone always leads to disappointment.
You'll be given "warning signs" of wobbly confidence and practical
suggestions for course-correcting your child's sense of confidence.
You'll learn how to guide a child to let go of negative thoughts and
move beyond any mental limitations to begin seeing himself or herself as the incredibly strong person he or she is inside.

Finally, I'll offer practical resources that you can refer to repeatedly. Each exercise is provided to spark your own sense of play and purpose as you cultivate your child's inner confidence.

*   *   *

Inner confidence doesn't happen overnight. The path to this deeper level of strength and poise occurs over many days, weeks, and years. Since you'll be living on Planet Earth anyway, these moments might as well mean something; make the ones you spend with your child valuable, so when you are no longer here, your son or daughter will still have the greatest gift you could ever offer: a sense of inner strength that he or she can harness to create their happiest lives.

My path to this deeper level of confidence is still unfolding. I'm both a teacher and a student, but I have come to a place of inner confidence—I truly know that no matter what happens in the outer world, my inner self is strong and can persevere. I am no longer plagued by feelings of insecurity, doubt, and a sense of uncertainty. Implementing the ideas in this book immediately pointed me in the right direction and transformed my life as well as my clients' lives. I am living proof that these Building Blocks of Confidence work!

It is my wish that this book empowers you and gives you the strength you need to cultivate inner confidence in yourself and your children—so all of you can feel a greater sense of inner peace and live your happiest lives.

part one

Confidence:
Here to Stay!

1

Inner Confidence ... Really?

Nothing splendid has ever been achieved
except by those who dared believe that something
inside of them was superior to circumstance.

—Bruce Barton

Staring out my window in Asheville, North Carolina, I watched the snow fall heavily down upon the trees. It was beautiful. But it meant there was no way I was getting on a plane for New York City that day. The universe had different plans for me. So I called my colleague, a bestselling author, to let her know I'd have to miss her event. What I heard on the other end of the line surprised me: the self-assured woman I knew was riddled with doubt, and in that wobbly moment, she turned to me for assurance.

I told her that her work was important, that the measure of her worth wasn't whether people showed up in the snowstorm to hear her or get an autographed copy of her book—it was something deeper inside that only she could give to herself. Our conversation was brief, but it had a big impact on me: I realized that no one, not even a bestselling author, is spared from doubt. What's important is how we use that doubt—and what antidotes we have in our "mental toolbox" to apply when it pops up.

Whether you are an auto mechanic, elementary-school teacher, soccer mom, or chief executive officer, the path from looking *outside* to *inside* for validation is a powerful journey—a journey that we're all on. It is the journey of the "spiritual warrior" that Caroline Myss has talked about for decades; it's what Joseph Campbell meant when he urged people to follow their bliss. Because bliss like this comes from bringing your unique inner talents out into the world—and that's a path that leads to real power.

This path is paved by learning to see yourself as strong and inherently capable to succeed, no matter what life presents.

The good news is that we don't have to start from scratch. People have been cultivating this deeper level of strength for thousands of years. What is new is gearing this information toward parents and focusing on how you can help your children develop this kind of inner strength.

Growing Confident Kids

Children are highly sensitive and develop rapidly; therefore time is of the essence. Making those years of early childhood as positive as possible will impact how they view themselves—and the world—for a very long time. With that intention, cultivating inner confidence becomes even more important. This process has the power to plant seeds of strength in your children not just for today—but for the rest of their lives.

Over these last few years, after spending countless hours with parents, teachers, and children, I've realized that confidence is generally misunderstood—in fact, parents and adults are often doing the exact *opposite* of what will build real inner confidence in both themselves and their children. We all have our children's best interests at heart, but with a little more guidance and focus, the same effort can reap greater confidence dividends.

I come at the topic of raising more confident children from a deeply personal place, and I've also married it to my profession. I had a very insecure childhood, and, as I grew, my sense of uncertainty grew—which brought with it a host of bumps and bruises. My deepest wish is that through sharing what I now know about how to cultivate confidence, more children can avoid that bumpy path to power.

Parenting Today

You may not always think of yourself as leading the way for your children to develop confidence and happiness habits—but you are. It is through the clarity of your example that your children's sense of inner confidence is created more easily and with more fluidity. This is why I will be speaking to you directly as a parent: Your personal example and understanding of confidence will set the course for your children's.

You probably already have some interest in cultivating a greater level of self-confidence in yourself and your children. The major reason is that everyone—parents, teachers, grandparents, stepparents, and kids—wants to be happy; and inner confidence—what we'll be speaking about in this book—is the prerequisite for lasting happiness. One of the outcomes of reading this book is that it will make the confidence-happiness connection clear.

Also, cultivating your children's inner world can only help in their outer life. Children who develop a healthy sense of confidence are better positioned for every area of their lives: they follow their instincts or intuition; they display courage; and they share their unique gifts with the world.

Outer Confidence

Confidence can mean different things to people. When I asked my electronic community of parents and friends what confidence meant to them, I got the following replies:

"Great hair day and my Bruno Magli high heels"
"Straight A's"
"I am confident when I stand UP tall and walk really strong"
"Mercedes-Benz convertible"
"Paying all the bills way before they are due!"
"Polished shoes, crew cut, and gold-plated cufflinks"
"An absolutely impeccably clean house"
"Making a flawless Thanksgiving turkey for twenty"
"A double-digit pay raise"

What do they all have in common? They're all based on external factors. That isn't surprising: the most common form of confidence is drawn from external conditions, like having a new haircut or wearing just the right outfit. When I'm about to speak to a large group, I always wear my Sunday best. This *outer confidence* is one step toward a more inwardly strong individual.

Is this what most of us believe confidence to be? Absolutely. Outer confidence comes from looking our best and surrounding ourselves with the things that make us feel *special*—like shiny watches, big-screen televisions, convertibles, and the latest touch-screen technology. Years ago, I was given a very expensive Breitling watch that I often wore to boost my confidence.

Similar things happen in a child's world, too. They feel confident if they have a SpongeBob T-shirt, special glow-in-the-dark shoes, and are wearing the latest fashion in barrettes and hairclips for everyone to see. These are all "outer things" that bolster a child's sense of belief in his or her capabilities.

The other way confidence is commonly created is by seeing yourself succeed at particular tasks. Acclaimed musician Sarah McLachlan captured this sentiment exactly when she told an interviewer, "I was a pretty insecure kid, didn't have a lot of friends, and was picked on a lot, and music gave me confidence." Sarah's story is like so many of our stories. Somewhere along the way, we discover that we had a particular knack for something—whether it was getting high grades in math class or playing guitar like a rock star—so we honed that skill and became more confident about it.

I've experienced this in my own life: I was elated to get a 3.88 in my clinical psychology doctoral program. It showed me that I could really succeed and could contribute original thoughts to the field. But I found that I *needed*—not wanted—to get high grades, so my own sense of self-confidence completely relied upon something out there (for example, how my professors graded my work).

We see this in children, too. My client Jonas began playing the piano at age eleven; within six months he was winning statewide awards. He was thrilled—it was the first time he was ever singled out for his abilities. If Jonas continues to play the piano, then this may be an outlet where he can healthfully create a sense of self-confidence.

But what if he breaks his finger? Loses a competition? Hits his head and forgets how to read music? His self-confidence will be completely shaken, since it has been rooted in seeing himself succeed at piano. If this skill is taken away—boom, his confidence falls apart.

This kind of self-confidence is rooted in seeing yourself succeed at a particular task or having certain things surrounding you that you've equated with feeling good. If you fail, or if things fall apart (for example, your house is foreclosed upon, you lose money in the stock market, you receive a poor report card, your spouse leaves you) then your sense of everyday confidence is lost. You feel adrift in the world.

This understanding of self-confidence is common in the Western world. Most people look to their things or accomplishments to feel inwardly strong. This isn't bad; it's just not reliable, since things can break, leave, or disappear. We need to use this outer confidence as a stepping-stone to a more lasting sense of inner confidence.

The Self-Esteem Story

What's the difference between confidence and self-esteem? *Self-esteem,* as you know, is a common term for feeling good about one's self. Western scientists have almost exclusively studied self-esteem instead of confidence—and there's a good reason why.

Self-esteem is a value judgment at a particular point in time. It's like a Polaroid photo of how you feel about yourself. Each of us can go through our photos and pick out ones that exemplify a particular emotion, like contentment or anger. At my college graduation, my aunt snapped a photo of me with a sparkle in my eyes. In that moment, I looked positively proud of myself.

Scientists like studying self-esteem because it's a discrete emotion at one point in time, whereas confidence is more multidimensional. Simply put, self-esteem is about liking yourself. It is also more measurable, since it's one emotional factor; confidence has more complexity, with both emotional and thinking components. Confidence is about believing in one's current or future abilities to succeed at a singular task or in life. A child can think confident thoughts and then also feel those feelings of strong self-belief.

My friend's son, Bruce, began recognizing words at three years of age and reading at four. His linguistic intelligence has always been impressive, so it's not surprising that he won the statewide spelling bee in second grade. Bruce practiced spelling with his mom every day for months before the bee; he was so sure of his ability to figure words out that he walked into the bee with self-confidence.

Again, confidence is a judgment about one's current or future abilities. It literally means "with faith" as derived from its Latin roots. Bruce felt sure of his abilities to figure out the spelling of words; he was confident about those skills from a thought and feeling perspective. Chances are, he also felt good about himself when he won the spelling bee—this would be a value judgment indicating his self-esteem. It is possible to have low self-esteem and feel terrible about yourself, yet still maintain confidence in your abilities to perform a task like playing the drums. One doesn't equate to the other.

Self-esteem and confidence are commonly used interchangeably, although they're distinctly different. These differences help us understand why there is a plethora of scientific studies about self-esteem positively correlated to factors like exercise, meditation, prayer, and community involvement, while confidence has been relatively unexplored due to its multifaceted nature.

The Path to True Power

Cultivating a healthy sense of self-esteem and outer confidence contribute mightily to the making of *inner confidence*. Inner confidence is a deeper sense of self-confidence; you find validation within *yourself* instead of externally. You no longer need external approval in the form of proverbial "gold stars" like the big corner office, a prestigious title, and designer label clothes to feel confident. Confidence begins to emanate from within.

When you have inner confidence, situations that would have broken you before don't have the same impact. You get fired, but it doesn't destroy you because you know you have the capability to persevere and succeed in the world. There is a stronger *you* inside who runs the show—and this is a more accurate perception of yourself as the powerful and highly capable person that you are.

You also no longer fall into the "emotional pit" of self-doubt and self-hatred when things around you don't reflect back to you your magnificence. Say you are an opera singer who specializes in singing Wagner's *Ring Cycle,* and all of a sudden your vocal chords are damaged and you lose your voice. This event changes your career, but it doesn't need to change your self-image. The root of "who you are" in the world isn't a sum total of your accomplishments or skills; it goes much deeper.

Inner confidence is the same experience for children. Little Lucy is about to take center stage in her fourth-grade production of *Where the Wild Things Are*, and she is fully dressed in her costume with dazzling makeup and hair. This is outer confidence. But as Lucy literally takes her cue all alone on stage, she must pull from within—her lines have been memorized, her sense of her ability to accomplish this task is set, and she draws upon this "inner confidence" that within herself she has the capability to succeed.

Eastern philosophy guides people to this deeper form of self-confidence, too. His Holiness the Fourteenth Dalai Lama explains it like this:

> With the realization of one's own potential and self-confidence in one's ability, one can build a better world. According to my own experience, self-confidence is very important. That sort of confidence is not a blind one; it is an awareness of one's potential. On that basis, human beings can transform themselves by increasing the good qualities and reducing the negative qualities.

From this perspective, *inner confidence* helps adults and children overcome obstacles, reduce negative emotions like anger, increase positive ones like compassion, and become inwardly strong so they can make a positive difference in the world. The idea is that without inner strength, you cannot become happy or useful to yourself or the world. This strength is square one.

From a psychological perspective, this inner strength can be used to live the life of your dreams. It takes real inner confidence to discover your talents and risk sharing them with the world. Your child's talents are like no one else's; they'll be unique and different, and your child will bring something new to this planet.

Eleven-year-old Olivia Bouler made headline news. She was broken-hearted after hearing about the Gulf oil disaster in 2010 and about how it negatively impacted the birds in the Gulf region. Olivia wanted to help, so she offered her drawings of birds to the Audubon Society to give to people who donated money in the efforts to remedy the oil spill. Her drawings raised more than $100,000 for bird rescue efforts within a few short months. Olivia had enough inner confidence to bring her talents to the world—and look at the positive impact!

Anyone can cultivate this kind of inner confidence. And the time has come for each of us—including you and your child—to embrace ourselves as the capable beings we are and enjoy living the life of our dreams.

Stages of Self-Confidence

You can create inner confidence. So if you don't feel inwardly strong right now, you are in the exact right place at the right time. And even if you do, nearly everyone on the planet can deepen his or her experience of confidence. Here, we'll explore the stages of confidence, from uncertainty (doubt) to outer confidence (certainty of particular tasks) to inner confidence (certainty to succeed in life).

Cultivating confidence happens as a dynamic process. You might take three steps forward, one step back, and then two steps forward again. It doesn't matter if you are a parent living like a monk on a mountaintop or a busy city mom juggling multiple priorities. The same is also true for your son or daughter. The key is to keep aiming your sights toward inner confidence and commit to course-correcting along the way. None of us are perfect, but with some skillful ideas and practices from this book, inner confidence can certainly happen.

The Stages of Confidence

Stage	Definition
Uncertainty	A sense of doubt about one's abilities.
Outer Confidence	A sense of certainty or assuredness about one's skills in a particular area. It may be something specialized, like playing soccer or practicing trademark law.

Inner Confidence	A sense of certainty about one's ability to perse-vere and progress in life. It is not specific to certain tasks.

Everyone wants to feel confident and move through life believing that they can succeed. The common challenge is that most adults and kids just don't know how to develop this deeper level of confidence.

That is where I come in, I want to share what I've uncovered from delving deeply into confidence from both scientific and spiritual perspectives.

So how confident are you today? Stop for a moment and really ponder this question. Below, I've characterized the stages of self-confidence to help you grapple with this.

Stage	**Definition**
Uncertainty	You feel doubtful about your capabilities. You have a repeated habit of self-criticism. You have trouble forgetting your mistakes and forgiving yourself for past errors. You focus on what's *not* right about you. You believe the negative things others have said about you (for example, "You aren't good enough," "You can't do it," "Who do you think you are?"). You question your ability to succeed at particular tasks. Things have a tendency to not work out, and you've begun to expect things to fail, whether it's a project or relationship.
Outer Confidence	You feel certain that you can succeed at particular tasks, like getting good grades, making an amazing strawberry-rhubarb pie, completing complicated tax returns, selling houses in a tough market, growing organic vegetables, or writing a popular blog. But you

Stage	Definition
	don't feel that way about everything—you feel deeply uncomfortable about your ability to make it through a crisis like a car wreck or the death of a loved one.
Inner Confidence	You believe you have the potential and capability to succeed no matter what life presents. When you're faced with challenges—like a flat tire, a bully on your child's playground, or a foreclosed-upon house—they don't deter your ability to persevere. Cultivating this sense of inner faith occurs by developing "correct perceptions" about your limitless potential and current abilities. It is not about perfection, but turning *within* for answers rather than seeking solutions from people, places, or things *outside* of you.

Outer confidence is the most common. The creation of outer confidence isn't "all or nothing"; you may have started to plant the seeds of inner confidence and are moving toward deepening that strength while falling back on outer confidence. These stages aren't 100 percent in one bucket and 0 percent in others; they exist in degrees on the path toward pure, unshakable strength.

Kids in Stages

Children move through the stages of confidence in a similar way as adults. They begin with uncertainty and then gain a sense of outer confidence on their way toward this deeper sense of internal strength—inner confidence.

Some of the signs of each stage for children include:

Stage	Definition
Uncertainty	Children doubt their skills. They are insecure about whether their capabilities are "good enough" and generally question themselves. They often shrug their shoulders, constantly look to you for approval, and often watch rather than participate.
	My friend's daughter, Jill, exemplified this level of confidence when she got on her bicycle for the first time and looked at her mother with complete uncertainty.
Outer Confidence	Children are self-assured about their ability to succeed at certain tasks, like climbing a tree, winning at a video game, doing cartwheels, or getting 100 percent correct on a spelling quiz. Their confidence is based on "outer" things, validating their sense of capabilities. But if they fail their spelling test, their confidence is broken. One of my clients, Collins, is absolutely sure of himself on the climbing wall; this is outer confidence.
Inner Confidence	Children display inner confidence by learning how to develop positive faith in their capabilities. They stop looking "out there" for validation and instead "see" within themselves the power and potential to succeed no matter what. Little Lucy stepping up in front of the whole school on center stage to perform was drawing upon her growing sense of inner confidence.

Children move through these stages in a natural fashion: A young toddler who is new to the world constantly looks at his mom with uncertainty. This makes perfect sense. However, if a child has opportunities to develop outer confidence but instead stays "stuck" in uncertainty, this is where more parental guidance and support is needed.

Inner confidence is also a process. It is a significant step for a child to move from outer confidence to this something deeper—this belief that within him or her exist the power and capabilities to succeed no matter what.

As parents, our aim is to guide children though these stages so inner confidence eventually becomes their default.

Myths of Confidence

Knowing the stages of self-confidence can help you create a mental landscape of the key markers—imagine it like an eighteen-hole golf course, in which the first hole is uncertainty. You have a clear beginning point and see the changing landscape and the endgame. Soon, you and your child will be thinking thoughts of inner confidence.

In the meantime, it's also important to debunk some common myths about confidence, such as:

- **You either have it or you don't.** Confidence is not inborn. It's cultivated by those who want to embrace their gifts, share their talents, and live to their highest potential.
- **Some people are naturals.** Everyone learns "tips and tricks" for how to become more confident in daily life. One of my friends is an incredibly successful Jackson Pollack–like painter, yet even he worries that no one will show up to his openings. (In truth, he always sells out!)
- **No one else seems doubtful.** Wrong again. No one is spared from doubt. It's a common human response to wonder if you have the skills, abilities, and power to navigate your way in this world. Learning how

to diminish doubt comes from recognizing your abilities and potential, while realizing that self-doubt doesn't support your dreams and goals.

- **Confidence is always good.** Nope. Children and adults can over-estimate their abilities (too much confidence) or underestimate them (too little confidence), which creates a confidence imbalance that manifests either as arrogance and conceit or a low opinion of oneself.
- **You must learn the hard way.** No way. It is possible to gain a sense of self-confidence and nurture it in our children through positive experiences and joyful endeavors. Surely, there'll be bumps along the way—but you needn't search them out.

Every parent and child learns how to become more inwardly confident. When Andre Agassi, the tennis champion, was a baby in the crib, his father hung tennis balls from his mobile. It was part of his confidence training that Andre could succeed in the sport of tennis and be whoever he came here to be.

Starting Out Smart

You were born with potential.
You were born with goodness and trust.
You were born with ideals and dreams.
You were born with greatness.
You were born with wings.
You are not meant for crawling, so don't.
You have wings.
Learn to use them and fly.

—Rumi

When you model inner confidence, whether you're a parent, teacher, therapist, or any adult, you're showing kids that there is a new way. The old way—to just stay in line and do as you are told— is a thing of the past. Our society is catching up to the truth that we're all born with greatness; this greatness manifests in our unique talents. Only with inner confidence can this greatness be brought to this world.

Inner confidence doesn't just empower children to explore their worlds and share their signature skills, it also lays the groundwork for their happiest lives. Children need this inner strength to lessen negative emotions (like anger) that upset their peace of mind and also to connect them with the ideas that plant the seeds of happiness. (The confidence-happiness connection is explained in Chapter 5.)

Raising children with a sense of inner confidence from the start is smart parenting. It saves children the pain and time of going down the bumpy road of having only outer confidence and seeking to please everyone but themselves. As a collective group of awakened adults, the time has come for us to raise children in a whole new way—a way that honors their greatness and empowers their dreams like never before.

2

Real Parents, Real Stories

The Chinese believe that the best way to protect their children is by preparing them for the future and arming them with skills, strong work habits, and inner confidence.

—Amy Chua, author of *Battle Hymn of the Tiger Mom*

Cultivating this deeper sense of confidence cuts across all cultures. Every parent wants his or her child to feel strong from the inside out.

In her book *Battle Hymn of the Tiger Mother*, Amy Chua shares her story of raising two Chinese-American children to succeed in the "outer" world. Her daughters, Lulu and Sophie, are exceptional by external standards. While other kids were playing tag, "Lulu won a statewide violin prodigy award and Sophia performed at Carnegie Hall at age fourteen," Chua writes. But are these children inwardly strong—or are they just particularly adept at pleasing their mother?

Hopefully, Lulu and Sophia will move from outer confidence (meaning getting awards, pleasing Mom) along the stages of self-confidence toward inner confidence (such as trusting self, avid faith in abilities, seeking own "north star" versus what is pressed upon them). The path toward inner confidence is certainly accelerated by seeing one succeed; however, inner confidence is not guaranteed.

Some of Amy's approaches with Lulu and Sophie are also controversial, and this is where culture comes into the picture. She uses harsh language, requires each child to practice two to three hours daily on their instruments (double time on weekends and no breaks on vacation), and forbids many standard activities like sleepovers, playdates, television watching, video games, and being in a school play. This methodology of emphasizing rigorous discipline, high expectations, and an intense schedule with little playtime is "Chinese" in nature.

Culture influences our perception, including how we parent and see the world around us. Every culture has its own unique ways of cultivating inner confidence. To learn more about how different cultures around the world cultivate inner confidence in children, I interviewed more than seventy-five parents from Peru to Timbuktu to discover the "best practices" in raising inwardly strong children.

I want to share some of those stories of real-world parents in this chapter for two reasons. First, they each present a unique culture and approach that inspired me. Second, they each have a takeaway that connects to inner confidence. As interesting as inner confidence is to consider and discuss, I believe you will find it much more meaningful when you can see how it comes to life in the real world.

Stories of Strength

Every child and parent has a story. As Joseph Campbell stated, we are each on the hero's journey—that journey of emerging through our tribal birth to become the person we're meant to be. Since there's no one else like your child—past, present, or future—your son or daughter needs to trust in the wisdom of who he or she is as capable, talented, and powerful in this present moment.

Some of these stories from around the globe helped me remember the strength of the human spirit as well as the amazing influence that parents yield in raising children to move from utter uncertainty to inner strength and confidence.

Third-Culture Kids: Developing Inner Confidence Through an Independent Childhood

> *In a funny way, when my son got shot, his inner confidence came through.*
>
> —Anne Goddard, President and CEO of Child Fund International

While interviewing Anne, I learned about her son, Colin Goddard, who is one of the seven college students who survived out of a class of seventeen during the Virginia Tech shootings in 2007. Overall, the college lost thirty-two of its students to a lone gunman opening fire on students in French, German, hydrology engineering, and solid mechanics classes. Colin was also the first person to call 911.

Four gunshot wounds led to the traumatic diagnosis that Colin may never walk again. But even faced with the emotional anguish of that possibility, Colin moved from being a victim to being an activist soon enough. Today, he is one of the most prominent activists in the United States for gun safety. When I spoke with his mother, he had just returned from screening his new movie, *Living for 32,* at Sundance Film Festival. He has said, "We live for the thirty-two murdered on April 16, 2007, at Virginia Tech and for the thirty-two people who are murdered every day with guns in America."

"I knew from the start that physically Colin could recuperate, and that emotionally he would be fine," says Colin's mother, Anne Goddard. She recalls Colin's childhood and how his exposure to many different cultures and ways of life instilled a sense of confidence in him. During his multicultural upbringing, Colin learned how to be flexible and adapt to new situations easily with a positive mindset; he tapped these qualities during his recovery. Anne's work as a Peace Corps volunteer and then with CARE brought her family to developing nations—basically Anne was working with the poorest of the poor people. Her kids are considered "third culture kids"—children who are from one culture (say, the United States of America) yet are raised in another (say, Egypt), thus forming another unique culture of expatriate kids. Colin was born in Kenya and lived in Somalia, Bangladesh, Indonesia, and the United States as a child before graduating from an Egyptian high school.

Along with this background, Anne believes one of the central components to Colin's sense of inner confidence is how she encouraged his independent spirit from the start. Colin was allowed to play with street kids, visit refugee camps, and go into other unusual situations to learn how to trust himself. Anne knowingly encouraged her son's free spirit and his daily adventures so he could learn to develop this sense of belief in himself. Each adventure successfully experienced developed outer confidence in his abilities to navigate situations, and then with time he realized these capabilities were inside of him—the beginning of inner confidence.

Many parents do just the opposite of Anne Goddard. They instill a sense of fear in their children. Moms and dads are afraid of their kids venturing off and possibly getting hurt; they don't encourage exploration and mastering new things, like climbing trees. They come from a place of fear, overwhelmed with concern for their child's safety instead of giving them a "healthy space" to explore, develop self-trust, optimism, new connections, and mastery over tasks. Of course, there also needs to be a balance between independent adventures and keeping a child out of harm's way but there is great value in giving children some freedom so they can discover their capabilities.

Colin's sense of independence and ability to learn self-trust down to his core is what helped expedite the creation of inner confidence. Little by little, Colin learned within every adventure that he could deal with all the different experiences in his life. He gained this sense of belief in his own power and strength inside of himself, instead of looking anywhere "out there." All of his adventures, from learning how to speak various languages (even if he did it poorly), to cooking new foods, to dancing traditional dances, strengthened his inner ability to know that within him was everything he needed to persevere.

TAKEAWAY: Confidence is created out in the real world—not at home sitting on the couch. It is imperative to give children healthy and safe opportunities to play in and explore their worlds so they can gain a sense of trust in themselves. Self-trust is the ability to rely on one's own inclinations (thoughts, feelings, and instincts) first, regardless of what others are saying or doing. It is also crucial as a parent to instill in your child a sense of self-trust, optimism, and avid faith in his or her ability to navigate new situations because soon that faith is internalized. Self-trust and self-reliance are necessary ingredients to inner confidence.

Hanuman's Super Power: Developing Inner Confidence Through Spirituality

You have a power within you that can conquer anything.

—Sree, Indian mother

Sree, an Indian mother, taught her daughters about this kind of inner strength through the story of Hanuman. Hanuman is a monkey god in the Hindu religion. This type of spiritual deity has special significance for her family. Her eight-year-old daughter, Neha, was being teased by a bully at school about her traditional Indian garb, spicy lunches, and prayers before meals; she was hurt and didn't know what to say back to the bully. To build up her daughter's sense of inner confidence, Sree shared the traditional story of Hanuman, the monkey god who possessed "super powers" to leap over buildings and display bravery when faced with fear. Sree suggested to Neha that we all have that same super power within us.

Immediately, Neha brightened up and seemed to feel more self-confident. No one had suggested to her before that within her was a sense of power that she could use anytime she wanted. Sree bought Neha a special Hanuman-themed lunchbox, bracelet, and image to remind her of that power on a daily basis. This, along with role-playing what to do with the class bully, has made a tremendous difference for Neha's sense of self-confidence. (Needless to say, the bully has since left Neha alone.)

Outer reminders like the lunchbox, bracelet, and image of Hanuman were things in the "outer" world to help Neha remember she was strong inside. Neha is still developing her sense of confidence—it increases as she "sees" herself successfully overcome obstacles like this bully. With some of these experiences behind her and her new belief system that the spiritual power of Hanuman is inside of her, the path toward inner confidence is developing.

Sree says that you must "first love your roots and who you are" to create strength of character. She teaches her children to love their Indian culture by sending them to Hindi language classes weekly, speaking Hindi at home, actively practicing and celebrating the Hindu religion, cooking traditional fare such as dal and rice, and connecting with other Indian-American families in the Los Angeles area where they live. This sense of positive pride celebrates the unique culture of India and also provides her children culturally specific tasks to master (such as learning Hindi language) to develop outer confidence.

Many South Asian families celebrate birthdays differently, too. When each of Sree's daughters turned one, she took the birthday child to the temple for a prayer ceremony to give strength, power, and protection to the little one. The family priest then cut the child's hair in four different places as an offering and subsequently blessed the child, marking a significant milestone. This kind of celebration goes much deeper than just a birthday party, and it connects a child to something greater than just wax candles to blow out. It plants the seeds of inner confidence.

TAKEAWAY: Cultivating a sense of spirituality through stories or personal experiences helps children connect to the power within them. If children get to "see" Moses, Jesus, Buddha, Archangel Michael, or any spiritual master portrayed in a manner similar to, say, Harry Potter, they'll be more interested in the ideas of the power of spirit. Sree modernized the ancient tale of Hanuman to become a contemporary hero who could leap over buildings as a way to teach her children that same power is within each of us. This is inner confidence in the making.

Refugee Strength: Developing Inner Confidence Through Family Time

My parents didn't speak a lot of English but taught me obstacles didn't get in the way.

—Joceline, Lebanese mother

Immigrants who've come to the United States, especially because of adverse conditions in their home country, are often able to more quickly develop inner confidence as a result of enduring hardships. Joceline, a mother whom I interviewed, shared how her parents came from Lebanon at the height of the Lebanon War in 1982. They didn't speak a word of English but had boundless determination. Her father, Jamil, was known for his cooking; with limited communication skills, he walked into a restaurant and asked to cook dinner for the owner. Within two hours, he was hired.

Joceline's father is the perfect example of both outer and inner confidence. He was confident about his cooking skills, but something bigger was at play here, too: Jamil knew he had the power to succeed. He displayed inner confidence.

Challenging situations demand that we dig deep within ourselves: It's only by going within and connecting to our authentic power that we progress. Joceline's Lebanese parents progressed from cooking for someone else to owning their own restaurant in southwestern Virginia. The idea is that we come fully equipped to succeed in life— especially if we can use challenges as stepping-stones to our success. Learning how to develop this skill is a theme throughout this book, since it is central to cultivating inner confidence.

Now, Joceline is raising her two children in America with a distinctly refugee mindset that turns troubles to triumphs. Refugees know hardship; those who succeed have figured out how to embrace it for growth. One of the reasons that I traveled to India to be with Tibetan refugees was to glean how they felt so good despite the everyday challenges of living apart from their loved ones while making due with inconsistent electricity, no heat, and limited healthcare options. I found that most of these people connected to the idea that troubles can be the seeds of something greater. They focused on their goal (whether that goal was freedom, abundance, health, or happiness) and used whatever showed up as a stepping-stone to their goal, instead of getting lost in the day-to-day details or appearances of what life looks like right now.

With this mindset, Joceline emphasized the importance of family and connection by sharing a meal with her family every evening. It's non-negotiable family time, where everyone gets an opportunity to share what happened that day, give thanks, and really communicate heart-to-heart while eating traditional fare like hummus, tabbouleh, toasted pita, and seasoned ground beef (known as *kibi*). This sense of normality and consistent encouragement gives children a sense of strength regardless of what is happening in their lives.

Refugees like Joceline's family know that everything can change in a moment. By having a set time daily to connect with family, such as dinner, there's a sense of consistency. A normal routine and sense of constant support by family members helps build inner confidence. Confidence isn't built in the sporadic moments of saying "You are strong"; it's in parents' habitual nurturing of children.

"You will always have your family," Joceline said. She's made it a priority for her children to know that her family is a pillar of strength, that they'll be there regardless of what happens. It is this regular family time where positive interactions are shared, everyone is encouraged, and a strong sense of belief in one another is demonstrated that helps a young family member increase his or her growing sense of self-confidence. This also provides a child a tremendous sense of safety and security in an ever-changing world.

TAKEAWAY: Children need consistent feedback that they hold an internal place of power, strength, and infinite potential. Joceline's family used the evening meal as the one place where everyone got together every day and became encouraged as powerful creators of their own lives. It is this daily bolstering of confidence and authentic connection between family members that helps deepen children's increasing sense of self-belief, sense of safety, and stability in this world so they can go forward to share their unique talents.

The Art of Inner Confidence

Cultivating inner confidence is part art and part science. It begins with learning the stages of confidence and gently guiding your child through them from uncertainty to inner confidence. Through these stories, you begin to see the creativity applied by parents and caregivers in raising inwardly confident children. There's no "silver bullet" or magic red pill to give children to make them confident overnight, but as you will learn from these stories, confidence is cultivated and strengthened in similar ways around the world.

Learning how others spark this sense of inner strength and guide their children to become confident from the inside out is the path of positive parenting. Now is the time to raise children in a whole new way—a way that empowers them to know their potential and capabilities from day one.

Confidence Across Cultures

The family is both the fundamental unit of society as well as the root of culture. It ... is a perpetual source of encouragement, advocacy, assurance, and emotional refueling that empowers a child to venture with confidence into the greater world and to become all that he can be.

—Marianne Neifert, M.D., pediatrician

Speaking with parents around the world confirms that the seeds of self-confidence are the same no matter where you live. Over and over again, adults emphasized consistent themes that nurtured their children's sense of confidence through daily connections, healthy habits, and creative freedom. Let's explore some of the recurring suggestions from empowered parents:

Family Meals. Like Joceline's story, the importance of family meals as a place to empower children was a theme that repeated itself around the globe, whether I was speaking with a dad in Indonesia or a mother in New Mexico.

One mother who I interviewed, Stefanie from Italy, explained: "The importance of mealtimes is ingrained in children from an early age. The appreciation of good, fresh food and time spent at the table chatting with family are central to the Italian culture. Food was not destined to be fast!" The lifestyle of fast food is typically American; many other countries seem to savor the sacred time of breaking bread.

One divorced dad from Canada shared a new practice he implemented in his household. John is raising three boys alone. Every morning after breakfast they hold hands, and he says, "Let's go out and give today. What can we give?" His sons answer, "smiles," "hugs," "a helping hand," and "jokes to make others laugh out loud." Playful exercises like this one serve a purpose and lead parents and kids to embrace their inner capabilities and help them see their power—thus seeding a deeper belief in themselves.

Creating the daily space in our schedules to connect with our children is important: It is in these moments where life is shared. Lily tells her mother over dinner about how her second-grade class got a guinea pig named Wilber; another client of mine, Anna, shared with me how she talks to her folks every evening at dinner about wanting to be a writer. The power of eating together seems almost indisputable. Children learn they can bring their successes, mistakes, misunderstandings, and questions to the table so they feel fully supported, especially as they grow up and bring bigger questions.

TAKEAWAY: Every child learns how to become outwardly confident by accomplishing tasks, but inner confidence needs more care and feeding over time. A daily space, like nightly dinners, can be a forum for fostering this deeper sense of self-belief; it is the habitual (not sporadic) nurturing of a child's deeper sense of confidence that makes it happen.

A Sense of Belonging. Over and over again in interviews, parents explained that they instilled in their children a sense of belonging to a family that loves them. Their language or location doesn't matter; parents, grandparents, aunts, and uncles seek to give children a sense of family. My personal and professional experience supports this notion. Children from loving home environments have an easier time developing self-love and self-trust, two of the necessary ingredients for inner confidence.

"What made me strong and influenced my ability to believe in myself was the fact that I'm close to my family, and I know that they will be there for me no matter what," says Daniel, a Brazilian father. This foundational sense of unconditional love is a powerful accelerator of self-confidence. Kids who come back to a family that is going to love them no matter what are more free to explore their worlds and risk sharing their unique talents.

This sense of belonging can happen through your family of origin, friends, or any type of community system. "Good friends are sometimes just like family," explains Denise from Denmark. A mother of five, Denise says that she has cultivated a strong connection with friends in her community, especially since her parents have died, and her extended family lives far away. Most of her friends belong to the same spiritual community of Buddhists and therefore share common celebrations, like-minded interests, and dharma teachings for children.

Charl from South Africa says that his "Christian beliefs have given our children confidence and a sense of belonging to the greater 'Christian family' worldwide. When we have traveled with them to Zambia in Central Africa or the United States, they have a natural affinity in connecting with their peers, whether they are AIDS orphans or children of wealthy families." This deeper sense of belonging to the human family connects people and empowers children.

TAKEAWAY: Confidence comes quickly from feeling supported in all ways. This type of foundational support can be from a family unit, spiritual community, social group, or other type of community. Providing children a type of "unconditional support" is essential in helping them move from outer confidence (meaning pleasing you and gaining conditional acceptance) to inner confidence (that is, pleasing and trusting themselves and feeling unconditionally accepted).

Quality Time Together. One of the biggest comments from parents, regardless of country, was to spend time with their children. This plays out in varying ways from passing down traditions, like woodcarving in Germany; singing culturally relevant songs in Lithuania; or sharing silly times, like laughing contests in the United States.

Throughout my interviews with parents around the world, I found that really effective parents spend time with their children in meaningful, life-enhancing ways. It is this quality time between parents and children that I noticed has an enormous impact on a child's sense of core self—they begin to feel valuable by your presence, and this is necessary for the creation of inner confidence.

Claudia, a Swiss mother of two, says "the time I spend helping my children learn the Swiss German language bonds us together and builds their courage in speaking." She makes language learning fun by sharing stories of her childhood in Switzerland in her native tongue.

Sports events are another major way parents across the planet connect with their children. Luis, a Brazilian father, takes his four sons to soccer matches religiously. "I love taking my children to see incredible athletes because I share with them that with hard work, you can do anything—even be a soccer star," he says. Encouraging his sons' sense of inner confidence that they can "do anything" with hard work came naturally to Luis in this setting.

Children want to feel heard, listened to, and nurtured on a mind, body, and spirit level. Some children will love spectator sports, while others may be more inclined to do puzzles together. It doesn't necessarily matter what you do—the point is that parents, grandparents, teachers, professionals, and any adults who nurture children need to spend time in their world.

Jennifer, an American mother of two, is an artist and natural creator. She has raised her children to make the gifts they give rather than buy them. Samuel, her seven-year-old, has made family scrapbooks for his folks, hand painted pottery for his teacher, and even learned how to sew a teddy bear for his grandmother when she was sick. All of these gifts were given from the heart and made with the support of his mother's time.

TAKEAWAY: When parents spend quality time with their children, it teaches them they are valuable, worthy, and loved. Children immediately begin to think of themselves as more cherished and capable inside if their mother, father, grandparent, or stepparent spends time in their world where they offer honest encouragement.

Many of my child clients had absentee parents, and this was a major cause of low self-confidence. Such children grow up yearning to feel loved and valuable, while often looking for it in all the wrong places (for example, making perfect grades to feel valuable or joining a "gang" to gain a sense of belonging). By spending time with your children in life-enhancing ways, you are providing them a necessary ingredient for the cultivation of self-confidence.

Freedom to Explore. So many parents suggested to me that when children get to explore their natural world with abandon—learn how to swing on ropes, swim in the nearby waters, and ride a bicycle— their confidence rises more easily. Because as children get to "see themselves succeed" in the natural world and master tasks like skipping rocks, they begin to naturally grow outer and inner confidence.

"My daughter has been kayaking on the ocean with me since she was a toddler and got her own sea kayak at age nine," says Melissa, a mother in New Zealand. Seeing her daughter Sophie thoroughly soak up the sun on the surrounding waters not only provides a great outlet for her daughter's enormous energy but also an ideal place for self-mastery. "Succeeding at something has immediately bolstered her sense of self-confidence," shares Melissa.

Raising children with an appreciation of Planet Earth, love of the land, and reverence for all of life is also a powerful teaching. "Kiwis have an almost spiritual connection with the land and sea," says Melissa. I, too, have found that as children connect to their surroundings and get the opportunity to explore them freely, their confidence naturally grows.

In Sweden, a law known as *allemansrätten* gives everyone the right to enjoy nature no matter who owns the land. This law encourages children to play in the streams, go tubing, pick wildflowers, run in the countryside, and explore the natural wonders around them. Glenn, a father of four, says that "being able to comfortably let my children run around in nature nurtures their soul and strengthens them."

Being outdoors and exploring the natural world accelerates kids' confidence. This may be jumping on a trampoline in the backyard or learning how to climb a rock wall with supervision—being outside in nature with fresh air and earth under their feet connects them more deeply to Mother Earth and provides them the perfect place for cultivating confidence.

TAKEAWAY: Connecting children to the natural world boosts their health and overall confidence in various ways. Maybe they get to plant seeds and nurture them into vegetables, or take Hula-Hoop classes outside in the town square. Recent scientific research supports that children who get to be outdoors more are healthier overall, due at least in part to the exercise and their intake of vitamin D. Seeing themselves succeed in their nature-filled adventures helps them create outer and then inner confidence.

Proper Etiquette. Parents and adults around the globe consistently commented about the importance of teaching proper etiquette to children. Many cultures expect children to pay respect to elders, learn how to eat a civilized meal, and greet people positively and with reverence. Etiquette also differs within various cultural traditions: you would never keep your shoes on, for example, in a Japanese house.

By teaching your son or daughter about proper etiquette, he or she gets to become more confident in social situations. This is outer confidence. But with time, this outer confidence can be used as a stepping-stone to develop a deeper level of self-assuredness.

"Children learn manners from their parents," says Jane Paterson, mother of two teenage children and founder of *1st Class Etiquette*, an organization that offers etiquette lessons to children. "Teaching them proper etiquette helps them feel comfortable and strong in social situations." Jane credits her childhood attendance in British schooling systems with teaching her the importance of manners.

Another parent, Claire, who is from Kenya, explains that in her culture, "Even a toddler as young as two is expected to greet adults and shake hands" with them. Cultures differ as to proper etiquette, but all agree that young children benefit from learning the basics of social niceties. Even in Tibetan refugee resettlement camps in India, Tibetan children are expected to properly greet visitors and show reverence to teachers. Teaching children the basics of greetings, dining, everyday courtesies, and other social skills helps strengthen their outer sense of confidence.

TAKEAWAY: Children who learn the basics of social manners are cultivating outer confidence—a stepping-stone toward inner confidence. The more children see themselves succeeding in the "outer" world, the easier it is to transfer that confidence to something deeper.

A Group Mindset. Many parents suggested that a "group mindset"— thinking of yourself as a larger part of a group versus surviving solely on your own—cultivates a positive sense of connection and confidence. Through my years of working with parents and children, I can say that kids who believe "we are in it together" have an easier time creating a sense of self-confidence than those who believe "I am doing this alone."

Anne Goddard says her son, Colin, "thinks of the group first, works to keep peace, and has always worked to overcome differences." Introducing kids to other cultures, either through travel, educational programs, themed parties, or culturally diverse schools facilitates a more collective, inclusive mindset.

Children's confidence grows when they see themselves getting along with people from different backgrounds. It creates a genuine interest in others and accelerates seeing their own potential and power on this planet. Martha, a colleague of mine, took her family of four to Peru on a volunteer vacation where they worked at an orphanage. "One trip helped us realize how much more we can give to others and empowered us to be there for more people," she says.

When children see how highly capable they are and see that they're able to do little things for others, their self-confidence grows. Imane, an Egyptian mother, shared with me that her children "enjoy the hajj feast of our Muslim religion, since they get a chance to attend a feast and afterward distribute the fresh meat to the poor with their father." The sooner children realize they are part of the bigger human family and have the power to make a positive difference, the sooner a deeper sense of confidence develops.

TAKEAWAY: Cultivating a "group mindset" in children facilitates a deeper level of confidence. The more children learn to think of and help others, the more their positive sense of self grows, and they begin seeing themselves as immediate contributors to the world.

A Spiritual Connection. Countless parents suggested to me that cultivating children's sense of spirituality strengthens them from the inside out. As children see themselves connected to "something greater," they begin to believe that something greater is within them right *now*. This thinking tunes them into the truth that they possess an internal power that can be used for good.

Parents around the globe shared their family's spiritual practices with me. "I sit with my seven-year-old daughter daily to say prayers together, make a candle offering, and end with a few minutes of silence to remember our inner peace," says Susan, a Nepalese mother. A ritual like this grounds a child and helps her connect to a deeper well of inner strength.

Simple acts like prayer before meals or bedtime and sharing daily affirmations or prayers every morning have a profoundly strengthening effect. Neil, a British father, says that "morning affirmations seem to bolster my daughter's self-confidence and really empower us all as we start our day." He shared his favorite affirmation: "I have complete confidence in God, and God has complete confidence in me."

Raising children to be "in tune" to their spiritual lives strengthens them in ways that can last a lifetime. It may be obvious, like daily prayers and affirmations, or subtle, like introducing a mind-fulness walk with the whole family, coloring in mandalas, or watching a TV program on a great teacher like Mother Teresa. A powerful piece of this puzzle is that children understand they are far bigger than their bodies and are spiritual by their very nature.

TAKEAWAY: Children who grow up with a basic understanding of spirituality are well-positioned to move through the stages of self-confidence. Spirituality isn't a magic pill, but through mindful prac-tices like meditation or study and prayer, children learn about their precious human lives and about the "divine spark" within them. Youngsters also begin to learn that by being born a human (not a toad, tomcat, or titmouse) they have a unique consciousness that can be harnessed to make their dreams come true. This belief has the power to expand a child's sense of confidence.

*   *   *

Hearing from adults about how they spoke to their children, encouraged them to master skills outside, connect with kids from other ethnic groups, and begin to believe in "something greater" were valuable components to the art of cultivating inner confi-dence. Sharing these real-life stories and recurring themes from my interviews with parents around the globe further inspired me to explore the creation of confidence.

Confidence has been cultivated across cultures since the begin-ning of time. Originally, it may have been confidence to start a fire from sticks, and now today, it's a little more advanced. We are seek-ing to cultivate confidence in our children so they can live the life of their dreams and become happier. My own background teaching spiritually based classes to children, guiding children and parents for decades, and creating curricula for emotional health across schooling systems inspired me to dissect the very essence of what confidence is and how it is cultivated in children today. In the next section, I'll share the science of cultivating confidence through the Five Building Blocks of Confidence.

part two

The Confidence
Connection

3

The Five Building Blocks of Confidence

*My mother gave me a sense of independence, a sense of
total confidence that we could do whatever it was we set
out to do. That's how we were raised.*

—Robin Wright

Recently, I was sitting in seat 5B on a very small plane flying
from Atlanta, Georgia, to Charlotte, North Carolina. It was the type
of aircraft where you see the pilot's controls from your seat and feel
the plane shake on takeoff. I silently prayed and readied myself to
sink into my spot in restful silence—until a middle-aged Southern
man in the seat next to me leaned over and asked, "What brings you
to these parts?"

His bright eyes and genuine interest to ignore the unsteadiness of
our small plane appealed to me. "I'm returning from teaching a parenting skills class," I said. He looked utterly transfixed. He introduced

himself and told me briefly about his background. Trace was recently married, and his new wife has two sons—now his stepsons—in their "tweens." So we jovially bantered back and forth until he asked what felt like the question of all questions: "How do I raise these two boys to be happy and go after their dreams?"

I spoke about inner confidence and how it is the foundation for every child's sense of lasting happiness, and how this type of inner strength also helps children pursue their dreams and get "tough enough" to persevere though any setbacks or obstacles that this world presents. Trace was listening, really listening. Soon the flight ended, and I sent Trace off with some new ideas about confidence, happiness, and the Building Blocks that can make them happen. He deeply wanted to know more about the Building Blocks of inner confidence and suggested that I write about them.

This chapter answers Trace's request—the same request I've had from many parents over the years who wanted a clear understanding of how they can develop confidence in their children. And as their children's role models, they wanted to know how to develop their own confidence, too.

The Five Building Blocks of Confidence presented in this chapter is a new model for understanding what confidence is and how to develop it in children. The Blocks are presented sequentially—a continual progression on the way to your child's deepening inner strength. (In the next chapter, I'll give you practical takeaways to implement this new model into your parenting life with ease and joy.) The goal really isn't to give you more to do, but just make what you are already doing a bit more effective in nurturing your children's sense of inner confidence and thus laying the groundwork for their lasting happiness.

Developing the Blocks

I began my career counseling adults, with a particular emphasis on healing childhood wounds. One day, it hit me: Why aren't I working directly with children, ensuring that they become strong and happy from the start? So I shifted to working directly with children and parents, helping them build this sense of inner strength and plant the seeds of lasting happiness. That led me to work in counseling centers, refugee camps, and inner city clinics, where I had the most opportunity to make a difference and refine my scientific and creative understanding of what the Building Blocks of Confidence really are and how they work together. From that experiential research, along with poring through stacks of scientific data on how to cultivate inner strength, resilience, and power, I developed the Five Building Blocks of Confidence. This is a new model for understanding confidence and developing it in children.

Basics of the Blocks

The *Five Building Blocks of Confidence* is a system that I created to help more parents raise children with inner confidence. There are many "hardwired" ways that people in the United States seek to feel good about themselves; however, they often don't look inside first. The system I will describe lays out the Building Blocks, or central components, to creating this deeper level of confidence that is grown inside and that has the power to propel your child beyond any outer obstacles.

In this chapter, you'll learn about this system and how each Block builds upon the next to create confidence. Ideally, you'll implement the Blocks sequentially as well, meaning that you'll start with Block

One: Biology, and optimize that piece of the confidence puzzle before moving on to Block Two: Beliefs, and so on.

Each Block of this system is important on its own, but when they work together, the deepest level of confidence can be created. Begin with maximizing a child's healthy body or brain (Block One: Biology), then steer his mind toward confident thoughts (Block Two: Beliefs), and supercharge those thoughts with high-confidence emotions (Block Three: Emotions), while strengthening his core sense of confidence through positive feedback (Block Four: Social) and a belief in something greater inside of him (Block Five: Spiritual).

You can guide your child to create inner confidence through skillfully implementing these five Blocks. If you want your child to develop inner confidence then he or she not only needs a healthy biology, belief system, and emotional core, but he or she must also experience the strength of being supported and connected to others. Putting these Blocks into play in your child's life will have a positive and lasting impact on the depth of real power and breadth of possibilities available to him or her.

Building Block 1: Biology

There is no formal education about the brain in
MBA programs, no brain-training programs at church,
no brain exercises in customer service or management
programs, and no real practical education about the brain
in school. The lack of brain education is a huge mistake,
because success in all we do starts with a healthy brain.

—Daniel Amen, M.D., author of *Magnificent Mind at Any Age*

Healthy brain development is the foundation of emotional health—particularly the formation of inner confidence. It is not even possible to begin cultivating a healthy sense of confidence without a strong brain. Most children and adults who are plagued by self-doubt, worries, anxiety, sadness, and uncertainty have a mild-to-large imbalance of chemicals in their brains.

Dr. Daniel Amen has observed tens of thousands of brain scans and images and says that healthy brains aren't like winning the lottery. You and your children actually have an enormous influence on how your brain develops; you can support the formation of positive pathways in the brain through:

- Proper hydration

- Balanced nutrition

- Adequate sleep

- Regular exercise

- Age-appropriate learning activities

- Healthy affection

- Nontoxic environments (free from secondhand smoke, free from fumes such as gasoline, and free from excessive television-watching)

- Healthy gestation (free from toxins such as alcohol, caffeine, and cigarette smoke)

- Limiting stress

These suggestions aren't just for children, either. Learning new things at every age, eating a healthy diet full of brain-enhancers (like fish oil and multivitamins), getting regular exercise, having a positive support network, learning to look on the bright side, and incorporating calming techniques like meditation—these are all amazing for the brain. (Science supports that regular sexual activity is good for the brain, too!)

Your child's brain is not a static organ that's completely developed at one point. It's always changing on a moment-to-moment basis as a result of what he or she is thinking, doing, being, and ingesting in this world. But childhood is the time when the brain undergoes enormous growth and begins forming initial positive, negative, or neutral pathways that relate to a child's sense of confidence.

Just having a healthy brain doesn't immediately equate to confidence either; the point here is that a child's biology or brain must be working for him or her if confidence is even going to be possible. I've seen firsthand the emotional disorganization of the brain with children who have been malnourished and repeatedly abused in physical, emotional, or verbal ways.

Samantha, a ten-year-old child client of mine, was sent to me because of her misbehavior in school and repeated thoughts of suicide. This was a doozy! I immediately felt I was in over my head and referred her to an M.D. for medication, since it was clear that she wouldn't make any progress without chemical help to balance her brain. Sam grew up in a household plagued by addiction, verbal abuse, and clinical depression, and her challenges were all normal responses to her early childhood. With new medication—along with a better foster home placement and one-to-one counseling—Sam's brain began to work for her rather than against her. (She was eventually elected class president!)

Recently, Sam sent me a letter offering gratitude for our work together:

Dear Miss Maureen,

Thank you for helping me in fifth grade. I really wanted to die and end it all—no one but you really understood me either. You were able to help me realize that it wasn't me but my brain that didn't work. So helping me fix my brain, exercise more, and eat better really changed so much for me. Soon I started to think better about me and made a new friend named Kim. I never knew that my brain had its own chemicals, and if it was off, I would feel sad and want to leave this world.

Thank you for not giving up on me. You are the first person besides my foster mom, Julie, that believed in me. I hope someday to make you really proud and send you a note with a picture of me and a happy family.

Thank you again,

Sam

This is just one of countless stories that I can tell of children who experienced loss, maltreatment, or abuse and weren't able to put together any semblance of self-confidence without first fixing their biology. I, too, was raised in a home rampant with depression, excessive stress, and verbal abuse; I understood her situation more than she knew.

Science of Self-Confidence

We really have a choice as human beings as to
whether we wish to let our brains be shaped
willy-nilly by the forces, which impact upon us or take a
more active responsibility for shaping our own brains in
ways to promote more positive kinds of qualities.

—Dr. Richard Davidson, director, Laboratory for Affective Neuroscience

In his research, Dr. Richard Davidson has pinpointed the part of the brain that "lights up" when you feel calm, in control of your life, and able to face the world with enthusiasm and peace: the left prefrontal cortex (PFC). Davidson has studied thousands of brain images and believes each of us has an emotional—or dare I say, confidence—set point. This is your biological leaning to "rest" in a certain emotional state, such as self-assuredness or insecurity.

Davidson's functional magnetic resonance imaging (fMRI) of emotionally distressed and doubtful people "lit up" the amygdala and right prefrontal cortex. The left side of the brain focuses primarily on systematic problem solving, mathematics, linear solutions, and, most important, controls feelings, while the right side is the more feeling side of the brain, where you intuit answers, act spontaneously, and are free (or less directed) with your feelings. The left side regulates emotions (like diminishing anger), while the right side is solely "free form" (feeling without direction). The more your brain leans toward the right, the more you tend to have a set point for unhappiness or doubt.

Thankfully, you can change that set point. Everyone can take a more active role in doing the things that help "light up" the left side of the PFC, so that your brain is working for you. Learning how to help your brain lean a little toward the left is important work to nurture optimum self-confidence. Active exercises that direct the brain toward self-confident feelings and thoughts engage the left brain's functions for emotional stability.

Biology is Building Block One and the foundation for all the future Blocks because it is here in the physical body that the basis of overall health begins. Once a child's brain and body are optimized, then it is possible for the thoughts and emotions of inner confidence to be learned and crafted.

This leads us to Block Two: Beliefs, which is about guiding a child's thoughts to become more and more inwardly confident.

Building Block 2: Beliefs

People become really quite remarkable when they start thinking that they can do things. When they believe in themselves they have the first secret of success.

—Dr. Norman Vincent Peale, author of *The Power of Positive Thinking*

Believing in yourself is a central component to cultivating inner confidence. You can only begin to believe in your capabilities and potential if you have a healthy brain and biological system (Block One). Many of my previous clients had chemical imbalances in their brain, such as severe clinical depression, which prevented them from being physically able to craft high-confidence thoughts (Block Two). This is why Beliefs is the Second Block: Creating confident thoughts and believing in yourself is only possible when you have a healthy brain.

After children's brains and bodies are "working for them," they can begin learning how to steer their minds and think confident thoughts. These thoughts will eventually be supercharged by the emotion of confidence (Block Three) and strengthened through positive feedback systems (Block Four). But the main point is that creating these inwardly confident thoughts is a pivotal piece of creating inner confidence.

Of course, I realize that thinking "I can do it" is sometimes easier said than done. It seems that we humans—adults, parents, and children—get stuck sometimes and forget how powerful, capable, and full of unlimited potential we each are. More than anyone, children need that help on a habitual basis to see themselves as inwardly strong and incredibly capable to succeed. This starts with learning how to create thoughts that produce inner confidence. (Chapter 7 provides a detailed description of how to create and transform thoughts on the way to inner confidence.)

Inner Power

The thoughts you think, the words you say, and the actions you take are all based on your core beliefs. These beliefs are always changing, which is good news: In every moment you can create your thoughts and form your belief system. Yesterday, you might have felt incapable of performing a new task; today, you may have shaken off that doubt.

Erik Weihenmayer, the first blind person to make it to the summit of Mount Everest, knows all about the power of belief. He was born in 1968 with a rare eye disease and lost his sight fully by age thirteen.

Erik's father, Ed Weihenmayer, always encouraged Erik to challenge the ideas of what a blind person can and cannot do. That encouragement empowered Erik and nudged him to embrace his power, tap into his inner strength, and fully believe in himself—to the point where he did things no one thought possible, from becoming the captain of his high school wrestling team to climbing the world's highest peaks. When asked about surmounting Mount Everest, Erik said, "I was confident I could do as well as anyone who goes to that mountain."

"If you develop the absolute sense of certainty that powerful beliefs provide, then you can get yourself to accomplish virtually anything, including those things that other people are certain are impossible,"

Tony Robbins said. I've found this to be true in my life, too. Not long ago I had the opportunity to walk across fire—something that might seem impossible to most people. It took me five steps to walk across a fire of approximately 1,400 degrees; in doing so, I realized that "possible" and "impossible" are very short distances apart and are separated only by our belief systems.

Steering Self-Confidence

The mind is a wonderful servant but a terrible master.

—Robin Sharma, author of *The Monk Who Sold His Ferrari*

Being able to direct your mind (your thoughts and beliefs) makes *you* the master, and the mind, the servant. No longer do you just accept ideas popping into your thought-stream and letting your mind wander onto subjects that suppress your power, create doubt, and diminish your sense of strength. *You* are the master; *you* get to practice and consciously create the thoughts that will result in confidence and certainty.

Cultivating self-confident beliefs means letting go of outdated (limited) beliefs and replacing them with more powerful (expansive) ones. One of my limiting beliefs from childhood was *I am not good enough.* I had the classic and common "not-good-enough-itis" that plagues so many parents, teachers, and professionals. It started when my mother flippantly said to seven-year-old me, "Why aren't you more like Sharon, the next-door neighbor?" I was crushed—a young child feeling rejected by her mother.

I began to believe that I was defective; I looked for clues that supported this sense of low self-confidence. It wasn't hard to find those clues, either: I received poor grades in math and didn't have a lot of friends. After decades had passed, I decided to ask my mother about this moment—one moment that changed my perception about who I was and what I had to bring to this world. Guess what? She didn't even remember it. As an adult, I had a choice to make—where should I direct my thoughts about this?

I decided to steer my sense of self-confidence into the sky instead of the gutter. There was no reason to hold onto my mistaken views and make myself a victim; after all, there are no victims, just volunteers. I believe that I did volunteer for this life experience, and perhaps this potholed path to power has been perfect for me to learn what I came to learn and share what I now know.

As you try to actively steer your thoughts in a more positive direction, you experience mental resistance. It may take many times before your mind gets used to (or believes) that you can do it, that you are a powerful creator, and that life is really here to support you rather than hold you back. Learning how to steer your mind toward inner strength and confidence is essential so you can actively guide your children to do the same. (Chapter 7 guides you, the parent and role model of inner confidence, and your child to transform negative beliefs to positive, confidence-building ones.)

Changing my story from seeing myself as a victim to a powerful creator took practice, and continues to be something I focus on daily. The more I consciously get my thoughts in order—direct them toward my strength, power, and purpose—the more easily my outer life seems to fall into place. And with this renewed strength, I find it easier to lead my children and others to this place of peace and power called inner confidence.

Beginnings of Belief

My mother said to me, "If you are a soldier, you will become a
general. If you are a monk, you will become the Pope."
Instead, I was a painter and became Picasso.

—Pablo Picasso

Parents have an enormous influence on how children see themselves. It begins before language even comes onto the scene: a child
observes and takes in the cues around him or her.

One of my earliest memories is of standing in my playpen and looking around at everyone while clearly thinking: *How did I get here? Is*
it safe? What's going on? These questions about safety and security are
there from the beginning; even if children don't have the words to
answer these existential questions, they're collecting the clues.

Language intensifies these environmental cues. A parent's words
propel a child's deepest sense of belief in himself or herself. Doña
Maria Picasso, Pablo's mother, certainly did her part to empower her
son; Picasso was known to be one of the most confident (perhaps too
confident!) painters of the twentieth century.

Sharing your unique cultural background with your child and
emphasizing your own sense of personal power can also shape how
your child sees himself or herself. Former United States Secretary of
State Condoleezza Rice, who grew up in segregated Birmingham,
Alabama, praises her parents for what they gave her. She said:

My parents had me convinced that even if I couldn't have a hamburger at the Woolworth's lunch counter, which I couldn't because seg-
regation . . . you couldn't go to a restaurant, you couldn't go to a movie
theatre but, they had me absolutely convinced that I might not be able

to have a hamburger but I could be president of the United States if I wanted to be.

By all accounts, John and Angelina Rice were ordinary parents—a high school guidance counselor and school teacher, respectively. But what they did for Condoleezza was simply extraordinary: their influence, both spoken and unspoken, encouraged Condoleezza to believe in herself and envision herself succeeding.

Charlie's Confidence

Charlie, an eight-year-old child client of mine, had a habit of saying, "I can't do it," or "look, I failed again"—which only reinforced his low opinion of himself. Our work together focused on letting go of those limiting beliefs and seeing himself as succeeding at tasks.

When we started our work, Charlie had just been named goalie on his new soccer team. I suggested he repeat success statements to himself, like "Yes, I can" and visualize himself actually blocking the goal as well as doing a little research on plays, and watching some soccer stars like David Beckham. He loved these exercises, and three months later, during the final tournament in Charlie's third-grade soccer career, he blocked seven goals and secured a victory for his team. Considering where he started—full of uncertainty—this was an amazing feat for Charlie.

Every child can cultivate greater levels of confidence with a healthy biology and a strong positive belief system. The point is that the Building Block of Beliefs is a central component to the creation of inner confidence that we'll return to over and over again. The thoughts your child is thinking will get supercharged by his or her emotions and become evident through his or her actions.

And that leads us to the next Building Block of confidence, which is Emotions. As stated earlier, confidence is both a thinking and feeling experience so after you have a confident thought it is also felt. The feeling of confidence is what intensifies the thought and it is here where a child learns how to rest in the "knowing" that he or she is capable, talented, and strong inside right now, no matter what the world is showing him or her.

Building Block 3: Emotions

Researchers have found that even more than IQ, your emotional awareness and abilities to handle feelings will determine your success and happiness in all walks of life.

—Dr. John Gottman, psychologist and leading parenting researcher

With a healthy body and mind steered toward cultivating confidence, the next step is guiding a child to truly feel the feelings of inner confidence. Confidence is both a thinking and an emotional experience. Any confident thoughts are supercharged by feeling a sense of confidence along with thinking those thoughts of "I Can Do It"—and boom, a child not only believes, but *feels* that he or she can really succeed.

Block Three: Emotions is a central Building Block of confidence. A common feeling of confidence is the way you feel when you walk out of the hair salon, and you look absolutely fabulous—you feel tall, look amazing, and experience a boost in your sense of self-esteem and outer confidence. This emotion of confidence intensifies your confident thoughts.

But this emotional experience of confidence isn't solely about feeling outwardly confident: it's also developing a deeper emotion of inner confidence. It's the feeling of confidence that is connected to the thoughts of knowing you are strong inside, capable, and able to persevere no matter what is happening in the outer world. The emotion of inner confidence therefore feels like inner peace, poise, and strength that is rooted in the intelligent belief in one's self.

Each of us is traveling this path of empowerment that includes learning how to create confident thoughts and feel the feelings of such skillful ideas to supercharge our lives. Another way to view this journey is to begin understanding the *Emotional Scale of Confidence* from fear to faith. You may remember from Chapter 1 that confidence literally means "with faith" as derived from its Latin roots; developing this intelligent—not blind—faith in ourselves is the emotional goal of confidence.

Along with learning how to move up the Emotional Scale of Confidence from uncertainty to more self-assuredness, it is helpful to remember that beliefs and feelings are different, too. Beliefs start in the head, and feelings start in the heart; both are connected to the creation of inner confidence. Confident feelings supercharge confident thoughts in children—so you want kids to feel the *feeling* of confidence along with having the thought. The more children learn how to join their mind (thoughts) and heart (feelings) together, the more genuinely powerful they become.

Are You Feeling It?

We should not pretend to understand the world only by the intellect; we apprehend it just as much by feeling.

—Carl Jung, psychiatrist and founder of Analytical Psychology

Confidence can be understood both emotionally and intellectually. As discussed above, both outer and inner confidence have distinct feeling components. Thinking certain thoughts spurs certain actions and feelings.

In early 2010, I gave a breakthrough talk to thousands of educators, administrators, and parents in the Philadelphia Convention Center on the topic of emotional education. This moment was a long time coming; with years of teaching under my belt, public speaking courses, and careful observation of professional speakers, I felt completely confident in my ability to communicate and offer my listeners practical tools to help them in their daily lives.

That day, my confidence felt like peace, poise, and power. I was certain I was the right person to teach about emotional education. I lived it and knew it from the depths of my being; I had years of both personal and professional experience nurturing children's health. The sense of calm that surrounded me on the stage was otherworldly and confirmed that my outer confidence was in communicating, particularly through speaking and writing.

As you know from Chapter 1, outer confidence manifests as certainty in particular tasks. My experience of confidence that day wasn't about assuredness in all tasks but solely an experience of strength in this one skill—public speaking.

Thankfully, I wasn't heckled onstage—if that had happened, then I surely would have needed to dig deep and find my inner confidence, the type of confidence that comes from knowing that all is well and remembering, in a tough moment, that "this too will pass." This was very unlikely but nonetheless possible.

Molly, an eight-year-old child client of mine, lost her father unexpectedly last year in a plane crash. In our work together, we've discussed how much she misses him, but to my amazement, she's said,

"I know that I'll make it through this with my mom, because we are both survivors!" Can you imagine? A young girl who has lost her father still knowing deep within her that she has the wherewithal to effectively overcome this obstacle. She's helped by her mother, Lillian, a strong woman with a deep faith in herself. I see Molly feeling her loss, crying when she needs to, and also standing in her truth of knowing that she certainly will persevere.

Molly's sense of strength is inner confidence in the making—and all children can experience this type of intelligent faith and emotional strength, especially if we as parents model this for them.

The Emotion of Confidence

Creating confident thoughts is a process children learn from their parents and key people in their lives like teachers, professionals, peers, and neighbors. Along with learning how to believe in one's capabilities, there is an emotional feeling that goes with thinking confident thoughts.

Let's take an easy example. My eight-year-old neighbor, Angie, is learning how to use a Hula-Hoop for the very first time. She picks up the Hula Hoop and gives it a try; when it continues to fall down, she says to herself, "I stink at Hula-Hooping," and feels uncertain. This low-confidence thought produces a similar-feeling response.

But let's try this scenario again. Instead, Angie begins Hula-Hooping and says to herself "WOW, I love Hula-Hooping and I am getting better and better!" This creates a higher-vibration thought and feeling right away. The type of thoughts your child produces, whether he or she is insecure or highly confident, will produce a feeling response, too.

Understanding that each of us moves on this emotional scale from fear toward faith—whether we are a parent or child—is what links us together. No one is spared from figuring out how to diminish doubt, move to self-assuredness, recover from feeling insecure, and move toward this deeper sense of confidence called inner confidence. The point is it is a dynamic process, and as we empower ourselves more as parents, we can lead our children to do the same.

This "Emotional Scale of Confidence" is provided below so you can see the "markers" on the way to inner confidence and aim your emotional rudder toward it. My experience as a teacher and student has always been made easier when I have seen the "big picture" so that I can stay focused on the big goal and realize every small step I take is a valuable part of realizing my goal.

You and your children can enter the scale anywhere from fear, doubt, outer confidence to something deeper on the way to having avid faith in one's self—this is the path moving toward inner confidence (see arrow pointing up). I use the word "scale" to represent that this emotional journey is akin to sound with higher and lower octaves of confidence. The peak level of confidence is inner confidence; although, on the path to cultivating this authentic power, your daughter or son may sing the song of uncertainty, move on toward crafting notes of outer confidence, and then with time learn how to compose his or her best song yet—the song of self-belief leading to inner confidence.

Emotional Scale of Confidence

Faith
Inner Confidence
Self-Love
Self-Trust
Optimism
Self-Assuredness
Outer Confidence
Certainty in Tasks
Uncertainty
Doubt
Insecurity
Fear

Inner qualities, like developing a sense of mindfulness and awareness, can speed the progression from fear to faith. Studying how successful people have traveled from utter fear to faith has helped me in my own path.

Viktor Frankl, one of the great psychologists of the twentieth century and author of *Man's Search for Meaning*, exemplified this. Frankl survived the Holocaust when the odds were clearly stacked against him; somehow, inside of him, he began to realize that no one could take his power—it was his, and he believed that the strength within him could carry him to a better day.

Each of us must travel this journey of empowerment and get as far as possible with our current capacities in this lifetime.

Charles Fillmore, the founder of the Unity movement in the United States, has his own story of going from fear to faith. One day, someone showed up at his door to repossess his office equipment because he'd gone broke. Charles knew fear wasn't going to improve the situation; with some quick thinking, he said, "My father is rich and always provides for me." The creditor decided to give Charles a few more days to pay him. Charles had meant God the Father, but the creditor clearly thought he meant his wealthy dad. Somehow, Charles got the money in those extra days, and nothing was repossessed.

This leads me to say something very important: You are what you think you are. If you come to habitually think of yourself as confident, you grow in your sense of confidence daily. You will also begin feeling the feeling correlates of confidence that go with outer and inner confidence. The point is that as you cultivate the thoughts and feelings of inner confidence in yourself, it becomes easier to guide your children to do the same.

I also realize that changing your thoughts from persistently negative to consistently positive isn't always easy either. Chapters 6 and 7 of this book detail how you can shift and transform thoughts that have been "stuck" with you for a while, whether they are old child-hood beliefs of being "not good enough" or other low-confidence causers. It is this process that can empower your confidence and can be used with your children to bolster their sense of inner confidence, too.

Sally Field, the popular and award-winning actress, stated that it took her a long time to stop seeing herself through other people's eyes. No one is spared from diminishing doubt on this path from outer confidence toward inner faith.

Outer confidence—where you develop a sense of certainty in par-ticular tasks or abilities—isn't a bad thing. It only turns unskillful if you stay there—if you remain in the place where you always need someone else's approval or validation, even though you are seventy years old and smart as a whip.

The feeling of outer confidence can also be smart or foolish. You can see yourself succeeding at particular tasks, which is a good thing, or you can see yourself mastering external tasks but desperately seek approval from others, which is foolish. See the difference? You and your children can use *smart* outer confidence as a way of cultivating the early steps toward inner confidence.

Moving UP the Scale

Emotions are a key player in empowering yourself and your chil-dren in becoming more inwardly confident. The way to move up the scale of emotions from uncertainty to avid faith in one's self is to keep up-leveling the quality of your beliefs.

Rick was a four-year-old child client of mine, and he felt very sure of his ability to accomplish certain tasks (outer confidence). Rick knew he could put together complex wooden puzzles, assemble a simple model airplane, and paint a birdhouse. Those were things he had done before and knew how to do easily. One day, I introduced a new project: We were to collect wooden sticks from the backyard and then create our own magic wands. I said, "Do you think you can do it?" and Rick shrugged his shoulders.

In this moment, I realized Rick was comfortable doing things he had already done before, but new things shook his sense of confidence. Since my background is spirituality and modern psychology, I shared with Rick some new ideas:

✓ Each of us has a power within us.

✓ This power is infinite and can help us do anything.

✓ You can access this power within you to create, do, and be anything.

And since some of my training has been in Buddhist psychology, I shared with Rick how Buddhists believe that every person has a "Buddha Seed" or divine spark within him or her that holds his or her potential to succeed in this life. This seed of potential and belief in your advanced capabilities is unique to humans. Dogs, cats, squirrels, raccoons, rabbits, and his guinea pig, Karma, don't have this power—just humans like him and me.

I kept my explanation simple so Rick could understand, relate the ideas to his own life, and then begin to develop a higher-quality belief, helping him move up the stages of emotional confidence from uncertainty to self-assuredness. Then, I went back to him and asked: "Do you think we can both find sticks now and make magic wands today?" Without skipping a beat, Rick said "YES!" and then we did just that.

There is no magic wand in the cultivation of inner confidence, but there is a "certain way" that it has been done for thousands of years. The reality is that cultivating confidence, especially inner confidence, is something that occurs over a lifetime and is a practice. Similar to a pianist who hones his or her ability to play symphonies, you are honing (and helping your child hone) your ability to create inner confidence day-by-day.

The next Block, Social, extends confidence creation beyond a child's body and mind to the connection with others. This connection is underscored as a vital piece of the puzzle that strengthens a child's growing sense of confidence and also affirms the power of a child's connection to himself or herself.

Block 4: Social

Research indicates that social and emotional skills
developed in early childhood are fundamental to academic
and life success, and in fact may be more important
than specific academic skills.

—Nemours Health & Prevention Services,
one of the largest pediatric health systems in the United States

Sound social skills—from learning how to resolve conflicts, play well with others, and other pro-social behaviors—are a powerful piece of a child's growing success. In this third Building Block, confidence cultivation goes from being purely an internal job (such as biology, beliefs, and emotions) to something external, too.

For children, interacting with others at school and home and during afterschool activities provides ample opportunities for feedback. When a child receives consistent feedback that he or she is talented, capable, and has great potential, they begin to believe it.

One of my mentors, Kathy Eldon, is the founder of Creative

Visions Foundation, a nonprofit organization supporting creative activists. Kathy has an incredible gift for being fully present with people and instilling in them a sense of confidence that they can fulfill whatever goal lies ahead of them. I distinctly remember leaving Kathy's home feeling that I could do, be, or have whatever I dreamed because within me was the power. If every parent, professional, and caregiver could provide children with just a wee bit of that sense, the global confidence set point would be off the charts.

Kathy is in the circle of people who I seek to surround myself with because they have figured out how to cultivate this deeper sense of inner confidence. One secret to doing this from a social perspective lies in having consistent reminders outside yourself (outer feedback) as well as internally (inner feedback) that strengthen your inner core of confidence.

By surrounding yourself with high quality, confident people and getting into a habit of building your own sense of self-worth, confidence comes naturally. Soon you learn how to speak the truth of your powerful being so much faster that you default to confidence instead of the opposite.

Confidence Feedback Loops

Confidence Feedback Loop is a term I coined to describe the necessary reinforcement needed to cultivate confidence. Specifically, these loops are circles of feedback consistently provided to a child, either from outside (parents, teachers, schools) or inside (internal feedback, self-talk) that shape their growing sense of confidence. These loops strengthen a child's beliefs and feelings of self-confidence (Blocks Two and Three).

The creation of inner confidence in children needs consistent care and feeding. In the beginning, a child's sense of confidence is fragile and shaky. But with healthy confidence feedback loops in place, uncertainty begins to lessen and intelligent self-belief starts to increase.

Whether we know it or not, confidence feedback loops are always in play. The two types of constantly occurring feedback loops are:

- **Outer (interpersonal)**—This is feedback from outside of the child that reinforces his or her growing sense of faith in his or her abilities such as school report cards, soccer trophies, or verbal praise from Grandma. Not long ago, my friend Maggie complimented her young son Eugene on his ability to dress himself for school, and he immediately was smiling with a sense of positive pride. Repeating messages like this on a daily basis creates a positive confidence feedback loop.

- **Inner (intrapersonal)**—This is feedback that our children communicate to themselves, either in words, feelings, or thoughts. Amy, a fifth-grade child client of mine, was incredibly apprehensive to try out for her big school production of *The Wind in the Willows*. It turns out she had a regular tape playing in her mind that she wasn't "good enough" to be in the school play. By changing Amy's mental tape—giving her a positive motto to repeat every day—Amy began to let go of her low opinion of herself. Before she knew it, she landed a role in the play.

Reed, my client Jack's grandfather, praises his grandson's growing ability to recognize words and put sentences together correctly at age four. Jack's favorite book is *The Giving Tree* by Shel Silverstein; he can already read the whole darn thing. Reed's specific praise offers Jack a weekly positive confidence feedback loop.

These feedback loops are necessary throughout one's lifetime. We often feel that we're only as good as our last win, whether it's scoring the winning hockey goal or making a fabulous Thanksgiving dinner.

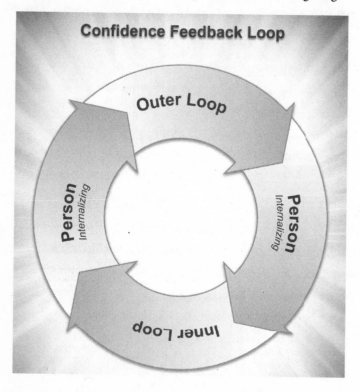

Confidence feedback loops strengthen a child's (or adult's) sense of self-confidence wherever they are in the stages of confidence development (from outer to inner confidence). A secret to seeding inner confidence is to place yourself or your child where high-quality confidence feedback loops exist. My spiritually based classes every Wednesday serve as one vital weekly loop for me; they keep me connected to a supportive spiritual community. It's my time where I get reminded of my power and capabilities. I also complement these events with daily loops of uplifting music, prayers, and meditation to keep me feeling and thinking confidently.

Both parents and children need to experience regular doses of feeling valued, praised, and acknowledged as being inherently capable with unlimited power. Some feedback loops my child clients use daily are:

- Morning Affirmations
- Mirror Exercises
- Spiritual Mind Treatments (prayers)
- Songs
- Movement (specifically core-strengthening)

In Chapter 8, each of these proven loops are detailed so you can start consciously incorporating them into your daily routine. Building self-confidence needs to be fun for your child but also must be done regularly—like working out daily if you're hoping to tone your body.

Outer Feedback

Champions know that success is inevitable; that there is no such thing as failure, only feedback. They know the best way to forecast the future is to create it.

—Michael J. Gelb, author of *How to Think Like Leonardo da Vinci*

Our world is always giving us feedback, like whether we passed our nursing exams or failed our driving test. Some obvious types of outer feedback are:

- **Words people say repeatedly.** These are tapes that play from other people: "Great job, Gerardo" or "Mike, please don't break another one of my glasses." Children receive these messages from parents and other authority figures every day.

- **Standard measurements.** Many children still receive report cards that provide grades from A to F based on a school's established grading system. If a child doesn't fit into an educational system easily, this can be damaging outer feedback. Other types of conventional feedback include sports trophies, competition awards, and spelling bees.

- **Things people do repeatedly.** Every week, the second-grade gym class at Christ the King School divides up into two teams. My friend's son Joey is constantly picked last; as a result, he feels physically inadequate. This experience is repeated weekly, and it sends messages to Joey about his level of physical agility.

Adults' outer feedback takes different forms: pay raises, promotions, prizes in your field, and other external marks of success or failure. Outer feedback that is most effective for bolstering a deeper sense of self-confidence highlights a person's unique creative expression (skillset) and talents instead of seeking to fit someone into a standard model.

Some more subtle forms of outer feedback are:

- **Visual Affirmations.** One of my child clients, Sonya, has a room full of horse statues and pictures of horses that she wants to have in her stable someday. Her trophies of succeeding at equine competitions are also proudly displayed. By seeing her dream every day, there is an outer feedback loop created consciously and subconsciously that affirms her goals.

- **Atmosphere.** Home, school, friends' houses, and other afterschool locations offer a consistent atmosphere of unconditional or conditional acceptance. At Lily's weekly gymnastic class, her teachers always smile and tell her they're glad she came.

- **Role Models.** The people around us deeply influence how we claim our power and build self-confidence. Are the people around you quick to praise your strengths? Do they see you as a success already? Do they walk tall and believe in themselves? Are they doing what they love? Children look to the "important people" in their lives to see confidence in and around them. The outer feedback received may be obvious, like verbal praise, or more subtle—like an approving, "go get 'em" smile that lifts a child's sense of confidence.

Subtle feedback is happening all the time, whether it is that smile, approving nod, or atmosphere of acceptance. By recognizing the varying types of outer feedback, you can put yourself and your children in the way of confidence-building outer feedback loops.

Nicholas's Confidence

Spending time with my friend's son is a special gift. Nicholas is an incredibly sensitive, smart, and irreverent eight-year-old, and like any third-grader, he is crafting his sense of confidence now.

I've observed his confidence deepen through mastering skills, teaching others, and then celebrating his success. We often play the free online video game *Wizard101* together; we gain levels, rescue lost souls, eliminate dark fairies, and deliver important scrolls. During our time playing, I get to observe Nicholas building his vocabulary, learning how to trust his instincts, and teach other players like myself.

After our sessions, we always chat about the wizardry events of the day, and I consciously focus on bolstering his sense of self-confidence.

Just yesterday, Nicholas said, "I love this game! I am so good at it, and it makes me feel great." It might seem completely inconsequential to adults, but these successes are a big deal to kids. Nicholas is learning that within him is everything he will ever need to navigate his world and that he can trust himself.

Confidence-Building Tips

- ✓ Go into a child's world
- ✓ Authentically connect
- ✓ Build trust
- ✓ Offer sincere and honest praise
- ✓ Stand back and see amazing results

Inner Feedback

Every waking moment we talk to ourselves about the things we experience. Our self-talk, the thoughts we communicate to ourselves, in turn control the way we feel and act.

—John Lembo

We're all consciously or subconsciously talking with ourselves. With attention, you can become aware of the things you're thinking or saying to your inner self. These thoughts can bolster your sense of self-confidence or utterly destroy it; the key is to become aware of this constant conversation and learn how to steer it toward inner confidence and away from doubt.

The earlier Blocks emphasized creating confident thoughts (Block Two: Beliefs) and feelings (Block Three: Emotions), but it isn't until now that we emphasize the significance of providing consistent reinforcement of these thoughts and feelings for the creation of inner confidence (Block Four: Social). Reinforcement can be external—kind words from a parent to a child—or internal, like a child's repeated thoughts. Inner confidence feedback loops are these internal conversations.

Children often will give you clues to the conversations that they're having with themselves. Jacob, a four-year-old client of mine, was so jarred by a preschool peer calling him "stupid" that he could not stop talking about it. Inside, he was asking: "Am I stupid? Is there something wrong with me? Why don't I fit in?"

Jacob and I worked together to heal from these hurtful words. I helped Jacob understand that just because someone says something doesn't make it true, and that he could stay connected to the truth of himself as incredibly smart, sensitive, and intelligent, regardless of what others say. Jacob also began to realize that perhaps his "friend" said a mean thing because he wasn't feeling good himself. With some mindful guiding, Jacob let go of his "low quality" feedback loops and learned to replace them with more skillful ones.

Most children will need help to create positive inner confidence feedback loops. Here are some pointers to steer you in the right direction:

A loop must feel *really* good to a child. Effective inner loops are also delivered in ways that speak to a child's leading intelligences (such as musical, linguistic, movement, existential, and analytical). For instance, my client Bella is ten years old and always has her iPod streaming into her ears. Since Bella loves music so much, her mom Rosie uses Francine Jarry's "Look for Positive Aspects"—an empowering song—to feed Bella positive messages in a loop throughout the day.

Morning affirmations or prayers are also a powerful way to teach a child about positive self-talk. Recently, I've been saying a prayer every morning with my family to set a course of inner confidence and positive expectation for the day.

Inner confidence feedback loops are formed through repeatedly hearing, saying, and observing oneself succeed. If a child's outside environment sends mixed messages or messages that he or she is not being "good enough," it is difficult to form positive confidence feedback loops. In these cases, it's essential for teachers, professionals, and other caring adults to skillfully intervene to guide a child to embrace himself or herself as powerful with great potential. (In Chapter 7, I'll offer a detailed discussion of how to help the "wounded" child heal from past hurts.)

Default to Self-Confidence

Whatever you habitually think yourself to be, that you are.
You must form, now, a greater and better habit; you must
form a conception of yourself as being of limitless power,
and habitually think that you are that being.
It is the habitual, not the periodical thought
that decides your destiny.

—Wallace Wattles, author of *The Science of Being Great*

Confidence feedback loops cause confidence by consistently sending your children messages that they are powerful, capable, and great right now. It's in the repetition that they'll learn to default to a position of confidence. The idea is that you nurture something over and over again until you naturally create a set point of inner confidence.

Perhaps you've realized that you or your children don't have many uplifting confidence feedback loops presently in place. That's okay.

You can always course-correct and consciously put you or your kids in places that empower yourselves on a more regular basis.

Years ago, I realized that I didn't have a community of like-minded people who supported me. This was an *aha!* moment for me, and once I sought out a community of people who supported my vision of myself as divine and powerful, things clicked into place in my life. We all need to be able to step back and objectively assess our lives to see where we're feeling confident and where we may need additional support.

A little time spent in honest self-reflection is essential for mindfully making the most of your social interactions and planting the seeds of inner confidence and ultimately happiness. I periodically review my life based on four quadrants: Relationships, Health, Wealth, and Creative Expression (including work). When I get clear on my intentions "inside" and create a schedule of healthy feedback loops in each area, then my "outer" life conspires for my success.

The point is that with effective confidence-building feedback loops in my life, I feel better and I have higher quality thoughts and this allows me to habitually guide others to the same empowered place. This empowered place is the goal for every parent and child to discover within themselves. This leads us to the last and final Building Block of Confidence: Spiritual.

Block 5: Spiritual

*The first spiritual law of success is the law of pure
potentiality. This law is based on the fact that
we are, in our essential state, pure consciousness.
Pure consciousness is pure potentiality; it is the field
of all possibilities and infinite creativity.*

Pure consciousness is our spiritual essence.

—Deepak Chopra, author of *The Seven Spiritual Laws of Success*

Spiritual teachers across all traditions emphasize that within us lies the potential to create our most fulfilling and happiest lives—that we are inherently spiritual, multidimensional beings, and as we claim that truth, then inner confidence becomes easier. We no longer look at ourselves solely as a housewife, plumber, teacher, chief executive officer, or author; we decide we are more than any earthly label—we are divine beings first, and the practical world around us is solely part of our earthly journey. Understanding ourselves first as spiritual beings with an inherent power and potential within us gives us confidence.

As you believe that you're connected to something greater, which is also within yourself, it becomes nearly impossible to see yourself as incapable and without potential. In his book *The Science of Being Great*, Wallace Wattles explains that the same greatness in the greatest people who ever lived (such as Abraham Lincoln, Mother Teresa, Martin Luther King Jr., and Babe Ruth) is the same greatness within you. Owning this truth empowers you, expands your spirit, and connects you to the field of infinite possibilities that Deepak Chopra described above.

Taking this truth and then teaching it to your children is where parents can spark a child's sense of inner confidence. So many of my child clients seem to be just waiting for an adult to see this power within them and encourage its healthy expansion and expression.

The Spiritual Block is also the last because it isn't *required* for the creation of confidence. It can be considered the "icing on the cake": it expands a child's sense of self-confidence and enlarges it to its capacity. The point is that confidence can be created through Blocks One to Four; here, in Block Five, that core sense of confidence can expand to its potential.

READER/CUSTOMER CARE SURVEY

HEFG

We care about your opinions! Please take a moment to fill out our online Reader Survey at **http://survey.hcibooks.com.**
As a **"THANK YOU"** you will receive a **VALUABLE INSTANT COUPON** towards future book purchases
as well as a **SPECIAL GIFT** available only online! Or, you may mail this card back to us.

(PLEASE PRINT IN ALL CAPS)

First Name _____ MI. _____ Last Name _____

Address _____ City _____

State _____ Zip _____ Email _____

1. Gender
- ❑ Female ❑ Male

2. Age
- ❑ 8 or younger
- ❑ 9-12 ❑ 13-16
- ❑ 17-20 ❑ 21-30
- ❑ 31+

3. Did you receive this book as a gift?
- ❑ Yes ❑ No

4. Annual Household Income
- ❑ under $25,000
- ❑ $25,000 - $34,999
- ❑ $35,000 - $49,999
- ❑ $50,000 - $74,999
- ❑ over $75,000

5. What are the ages of the children living in your house?
- ❑ 0 - 14 ❑ 15+

6. Marital Status
- ❑ Single
- ❑ Married
- ❑ Divorced
- ❑ Widowed

7. How did you find out about the book?
(please choose one)
- ❑ Recommendation
- ❑ Store Display
- ❑ Online
- ❑ Catalog/Mailing
- ❑ Interview/Review

8. Where do you usually buy books?
(please choose one)
- ❑ Bookstore
- ❑ Online
- ❑ Book Club/Mail Order
- ❑ Price Club (Sam's Club, Costco's, etc.)
- ❑ Retail Store (Target, Wal-Mart, etc.)

9. What subject do you enjoy reading about the most?
(please choose one)
- ❑ Parenting/Family
- ❑ Relationships
- ❑ Recovery/Addictions
- ❑ Health/Nutrition
- ❑ Christianity
- ❑ Spirituality/Inspiration
- ❑ Business Self-help
- ❑ Women's Issues
- ❑ Sports

10. What attracts you most to a book?
(please choose one)
- ❑ Title
- ❑ Cover Design
- ❑ Author
- ❑ Content

TAPE IN MIDDLE; DO NOT STAPLE

I₁lI₁₁II₁l₁₁l₁lI₁l₁l₁llI₁l₁l₁l₁₁l₁lI₁l₁lI

FOLD HERE

Comments

Science of Spirituality

To make children happier, we may need to encourage them
to develop a strong sense of personal worth, according to
Dr. Mark Holder from the University of British Columbia
in Canada and his colleagues Dr. Ben Coleman and Judi
Wallace. Their research shows that children who feel that
their lives have meaning and value and who
develop deep, quality relationships—both measures
of spirituality—are happier.

—*Science Daily* (www.sciencedaily.com), a news website for science articles

Scientists and scholars have long established the positive link between spirituality and happiness. Dr. Mark Holder, associate professor at the University of British Columbia, recently studied the impact of spirituality in the lives of elementary-aged children in Canada and then again in New Delhi, India. He found that children who believed in themselves (confidence) and considered themselves to be spiritual (through prayers, meditating, or talking to God) were happier.

In his study, spirituality was defined as distinctly different from religion. Practicing religion was comprised of things like attending church weekly and participating in rituals like First Communion, whereas spirituality was more of a belief in "a higher power," whether it was termed "God" or something else. The study didn't find any positive correlation between religiosity and happiness.

Holder's study also didn't find money, gender, or a parents' marital status as accounting for happiness. It appears that a child's sense of happiness isn't based on things "out there" but is comprised of cultivating a richness "inside" that is deeper and more connected to transcendental things, like faith, belief in a higher power, value of one's life and core self, sense of awe for this world, and depth of personal relationships.

These same things that help spur a sense of happiness in children are only created when a child believes in himself or herself. Connecting to the spiritual side of life often helps accelerate a child's understanding that within him or her there is a power and strength beyond any scientific understanding.

The Spiritual Side

Let go, and let God.

—Alcoholics Anonymous Motto

Our lives provide us ample opportunities to grow into our spiritual birthright as powerful creators and channels for the divine. Instead of seeking to constantly be in control, the spiritual path teaches us to surrender to the present moment, however it appears. The recovery movement has a saying that is fitting: there comes a point when it is skillful to "Let go, and let God," meaning that to overcome some earthly obstacles, assistance from the divine is the fastest and easiest path to a surefire solution.

This belief in a "higher power" or divine solution to any situation is taught differently in various traditions and philosophies. Despite these differences, many of the fundamental truths remain the same; many spiritual paths lead to a deeper and more meaningful belief in one's self. Contemporary Christianity teaches that each of us has the "Christ Consciousness" within ourselves. This is the divine spark that can lead to inner confidence and a sense of heightened awareness. St. Teresa of Avila explained that sometimes, "We don't remember we are creatures made in the image of God. We don't understand the great secrets hidden in us."

Similarly, Buddhism teaches that every human being is born with a "Buddha Seed"—the potential within for emotional freedom, inner peace, and ultimately happiness. Buddha was the "awakened one" who provided teachings and served as a great spiritual master akin to Jesus.

Realizing your potential from a spiritual perspective allows you to see yourself as equal with others and provide yourself much needed and deserved self-love. "You can search throughout the entire universe for someone who is more deserving of your love and affection than you are yourself, and that person is not to be found anywhere. You yourself, as much as anybody in the entire universe, deserve your love and affection," explained the Buddha. Loving one's self is a spiritual exercise in nonjudgment and unconditional acceptance that strengthens one's sense of confidence. As you continue to deepen your sense of self-love and confidence, you can more clearly teach your son or daughter to do the same.

Sree, the Indian mother mentioned in the last chapter, led her children to more fully believe in themselves through her spiritual tradition and the belief that within them is a great power—and her kids became more inwardly confident. This type of teaching helps children strengthen their sense of inner confidence.

Connecting the Blocks

The Five Building Blocks of Confidence are interconnected; each one plays a pivotal role in developing confidence from outer to inner. This system starts with optimizing a child's biology or body and then focuses on his or her mind, which must be trained to develop thoughts of inner confidence. These thoughts are then amplified through confident feelings. This marriage of inwardly confident thoughts and feelings leads to real power and choices that a child can be proud of. No longer does a child need to constantly be seeking approval from "out there" but can learn to look within for guidance and strength.

Then, with this starter level of confidence, every child needs it strengthened through outer feedback to help him or her begin uplifting self-talk, which feeds that growing sense of self-confidence.

The belief in something greater is the last piece of the confidence puzzle; around the planet, parents and children maximize their sense of confidence from outer to inner through believing in a spiritual power within them that can be used for good.

The first four Building Blocks working optimally are absolutely necessary to create inner confidence; the Spiritual Block is a source for many—but not all—that spurs a deeper connection to the power within and helps expand a child's notion of confidence beyond any previous limitations.

The Five Building Blocks of Confidence is visually depicted here to help you "see" how they each work and understand their roles:

Building Block One: Biology   Child's Healthy Body and Brain
                                           Foundation of Confidence

Building Block Two: Beliefs   Confident Thoughts
                                           Creator of Confidence

Building Block Three: Emotions   Confident Feelings
                                           Amplifier of Confident Thoughts

Building Block Four: Social Outer and Inner Feedback
Strengthener of Thoughts
and Feelings

Building Block Five: Spiritual Belief in Something Greater
Expander of Confidence

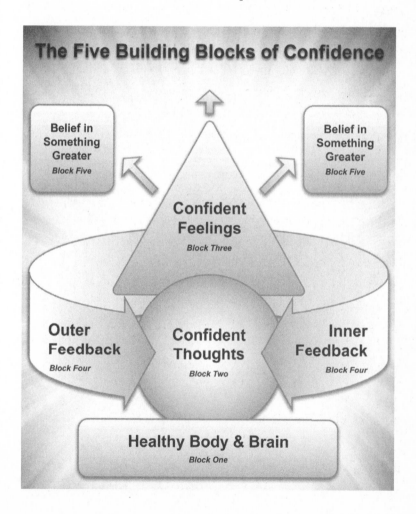

The Five Building Blocks of Confidence

Belief in Something Greater
Block Five

Belief in Something Greater
Block Five

Confident Feelings
Block Three

Outer Feedback
Block Four

Confident Thoughts
Block Two

Inner Feedback
Block Four

Healthy Body & Brain
Block One

4

Bringing the Blocks to Life

*If you ask any great player or great quarterback, there's a
certain inner confidence that you're as good as anybody.*

—Dan Marino, Football Hall of Fame quarterback

As I walked along the creek by my office with Isabel, an eight-year-old client, I turned to her and asked, "Do you know what confidence is?" She smiled and quickly said, "Yes" as if she was being tested. I knew from her certainty and positive response that progress had been made in the previous few months. Jose, her father, started bringing Isabel to me because of some recent school trouble: she was being teased for her small stature, Spanish accent, and "smelly" lunches since most kids brought peanut butter sandwiches.

"When I believe in myself is confidence," Isabel explained to me. I agreed with Isabel but still wondered if she "felt" confident at certain points, so I inquired, "When do you feel confident?" Without hesitation, Isabel replied:

I am confident about EOG's (end of year grades) and my singing. My friends, parents, and other people tell me I am an excellent singer. I just need to record myself and put it on *YouTube* [the website]. That's how most people get discovered these days—not in a garage band anymore.

Isabel's response was a strong one. She no longer worried about being different because of her below-average height or Spanish accent. I worked with Isabel to see her differences as strengths, celebrate them, and focus on developing her natural gifts into real skills, like taking singing lessons. In conjunction with working with Isabel, I met with her parents weekly to explain the Five Building Blocks of Confidence and how they play a role in cultivating Isabel's self-confidence.

As Isabel began getting more sleep and better daily nutrition (Block One), along with seeing herself as talented and capable right now (Block Two), her feelings changed and became stronger, and she didn't crumble in the face of her teasing peers (Block Three). Her parents, Jose and Maria, also signed up Isabel for weekly singing lessons, providing her an invaluable way to receive consistent and confidence-building feedback (Block Four). With each step forward in succeeding at school or singing, Isabel's natural sense of confidence increased, and she was no longer bothered by her peers.

Seeing how the Five Building Blocks of Confidence "came to life" in Isabel's situation and learning how to animate them for your child is the topic of this chapter. It goes beyond the basics of the five Blocks to focus you on *how* they can become powerful forces for your child's growing sense of confidence.

Beyond the Basics

Understanding the Building Blocks of Confidence is step one. It is similar to taking out all the ingredients to bake a cake: You know you'll need milk, sugar, butter, flour, and so forth. They are necessary ingredients, but how the cake "turns out" depends upon how you put these ingredients together and let them work.

Isabel's parents understood the Building Blocks of Confidence and began putting them together so Isabel's confidence would grow naturally. Her confidence skyrocketed when she had *personal experience* in seeing herself succeed. This is an important point. Your child needs to experience his or her power directly and begin seeing success at something.

There is no shortcut for personal experience. Think of yourself. Remember a time when you wanted to master a task—say, hitting the tennis ball over the net. You began by learning how to hold the racquet, stand in proper position, and swing at the tennis ball so it would be returned to your opponent. As you began successfully hitting the tennis ball and it was going in the right direction, you started to think "Wow, I can do this" and "Perhaps this sport isn't as hard as it looks."

Your child's growing sense of confidence happens the same way. I can remember just last week that my friend's son Nicholas came over saying, "I got the highest EOG grade!" and was clearly thrilled. By his own experience, he is gaining a sense of confidence in his ability to learn new things, pass tests, and succeed academically. This is outer confidence.

The Five Building Blocks of Confidence come alive through personal experience, too. Each Block plays a vital role in nurturing a growing child's sense of confidence. When each of the Blocks is working optimally, they point a child toward inner confidence and build upon outer confidence.

Experience Plus Wisdom

Along with direct experience, a child who learns how to "ground" his or her thinking in wise ideas has the second secret of planting the seeds of inner confidence.

Emma, my friend's ten-year-old daughter, is the perfect example of this point. She has been taking horseback riding lessons for the last three years and just recently started competing with her horse, Lovey. Emma started placing in competitions with her horse from the beginning; she attributes part of her success to the time spent on the horse.

Interestingly enough, she says the other part of her success is "how I think about each day and doing my best possible." Her mother, Trish, sits with Emma every morning to claim her greatness and remember her power in the words of Ernest Holmes. They recite this prayer together:

> I know that within myself there is that Life, which is Perfect, Complete and Divine; It was never born and cannot die, for it lives and is God. Within myself is the Wholeness, Peace, Poise and Power of Life. This Life is Health, It is Abundance, It is Love. There is One Life and it is the Life of God and this is my Life Now!

Such a prayer reminds Emma on a daily basis that she is powerful and that within her is the divine spark of God. It is from this place that she moves forward, knowing that through her positive thoughts, affirmations, and beliefs she can create whatever she chooses each day—and with Lovey she chooses to do her best. Once I asked Emma, "Do you place every time you enter a competition?" and she quickly replied, "No, but I always do my best," and this is a powerful knowing for a young child.

Trish and Emma are students of the Science of Mind teachings as founded by Ernest Holmes, which empowers people to believe that through your thoughts you create your life. I also agree that thought is the most powerful force in the universe. You needn't be a student of Science of Mind though—the important point is to anchor your child's emerging sense of confidence in himself or herself through positive thinking that resonates with both of you . . . and that can be through cultural stories, myths, or spiritual traditions.

Previously, I shared that my *aha!* moment with inner confidence came once I connected with Buddhist philosophy and how it teaches that every person has the power within them to succeed merely by being born a human. It was here where my mind was trained to see my inner power first and foremost instead of any perceived weaknesses. Compelled by this teaching, I then began teaching young children about their inner confidence.

So my suggestion is to find something that empowers you as a parent or teacher, and then teach that to your child. Your son or daughter will not only be taught by your words but feel your enthusiasm—so go light yourself up.

Moving Forward

Within this chapter we move forward, focused on how to bring the Five Building Blocks of Confidence alive for your child . . . especially with the knowing that:

- **Personal Experience Is Power.** It is only through a child's direct experience that he comes to believe in himself fully. Your role as a parent is to provide your child with opportunities to experience his or her power physically (Block One), mentally (Block Two), emotionally (Block Three), socially (Block Four), and spiritually (Block Five) so that confidence arises naturally.

- **Positive Thinking Is the Anchor.** Along with providing your child direct experiences where he or she begins "seeing" their capabilities, you need to be an example of positive and empowering thoughts— and also teach such thinking to your child. You get to choose how to ground your thinking, too, whether it is in New Thought, Buddhism, Christianity, New Age, Judaism, or other teachings.

With these two key insights in mind, we can now activate the Five Building Blocks of Confidence in a greater way. You no longer see the Blocks as a two-dimensional idea but can see them animated in our 3-D world. Being a parent of power and providing your child those experiences to see his or her power becomes foremost in your mind.

Implementing Block One: Biology

Building Block One: Biology is the foundation of the Five Building Blocks of Confidence. It underscores the importance of a child's biology (brain and body) as the basis of his or her emotional and mental health. Without their brains "working for them," children cannot cultivate inner confidence.

Busy parents and adults (me, too!) can easily overlook brain health by forgetting to ensure our children get:

- ✓ Regular exercise
- ✓ Adequate sleep
- ✓ Healthy nutrition
- ✓ Proper hydration
- ✓ Healthy hugs (and affection)

Physical Activity

Getting regular physical exercise is essential for a child's growing system: it helps them build strong bodies (muscles and bones), gain a sense of physical mastery, releases natural opiates (feel-good chemicals), and uses up stress chemicals like adrenaline that their bodies generate at times such as pop spelling quizzes.

The type of physical activity that is of benefit depends on the child. One child client of mine, Alexis, is not that interested in team sports, but she loves the outdoors. So I suggested to her mother that perhaps Alexis could start a garden: getting and tilling the best soil, finding the seeds, planting them, and caring for her crop. Alexis and her mom loved this idea, and without realizing it, Alexis was getting a lot of exercise—using a rake and hoe, digging in the dirt, and putting up a fence.

Not every child is going to be an athlete, and that's absolutely acceptable. Finding and matching children to some sort of physical activity that they enjoy and can use to strengthen their bodies is extremely beneficial. Sometimes it also takes a little creativity: Alexis didn't want to play basketball, but putting her outside was magical. It was in complete alignment to her true self—a child who loves nature and wants to nurture plants.

The more adults take time to pay attention to children's interests, the easier it becomes to match a child to proper physical activity. Some other not-so-obvious types of exercise include:

- ✓ Building a tree house
- ✓ Cooking with parents
- ✓ Sharing a cooperative garden
- ✓ Jumping on a trampoline
- ✓ Redecorating a room (including painting and spring cleaning)
- ✓ Helping with a yard sale

Anything that moves energy through the body works: soccer, baseball, ballet, drumming lessons, acting in plays, pottery classes, gymnastics, swimming, yoga, tai chi, clogging—literally anything. Children are naturally energetic; if they don't have good physical outlets, that energy is trapped and can manifest in less optimal ways such as yelling, kicking, screaming, hitting, and more.

Your role here is to give your child an outlet for energy and an opportunity to develop physical strength, master tasks, and begin seeing himself or herself succeed, whether it is at soccer or playing the piano. Remember, it is the personal experience of succeeding that begins building a child's sense of confidence.

Sleep

Many kids don't get enough rest for a variety of reasons: Maybe there was a great football game on nighttime television, or maybe divorced parents don't enforce the same bedtime in their respective homes. Sleep is a necessity, not a luxury; during those hours, a child's brain is reorganizing the events of the day, reviewing new skills of self-confidence learned from the day, and restoring the body to a natural state of optimum health. I am always surprised when I visit a classroom and see child after child with bags under their eyes, struggling to stay awake.

Here are some bedtime suggestions for parents from the Nemours Foundation, a nonprofit organization dedicated to improving the health of children:

- Set a consistent bedtime
- Remind children to start winding down thirty minutes before bedtime
- Suggest a trip to the bathroom (brushing teeth, washing up, and shower time)
- Provide a comfortable sleep space (night-light, teddy bear, cozy pillows

and comforter, photos of family, gentle relaxation music, and calming crystals)
- Offer consistent sleep time rituals (children's book or story time)
- Be positive in the morning (if things went really well, praise your kids!)

Setting a routine and making the child safe and comfortable in their sleep patterns is of paramount importance—especially if a child is dealing with an emotional situation like divorce, loss, or any other upset.

Sleep is also a necessary ingredient for children to feel strong inside. The creation of inner confidence can only happen when their bodies are well-rested and their brains are working for them. (Remember a time when you were sleep deprived and how that impacted everything—often, not for the better.)

Healthy Nutrition

Working with children globally, I have had a firsthand opportunity to be with young kids who don't receive proper nutrition daily . . . and I've seen the consequences. In India, I met the sweetest boy whose name was Tenzin. I adored him, and he sat on my lap every day for three months. Because of his family situation, Tenzin ate a poor diet—mostly cookies for breakfast, candy for snacks, rice for lunch, and soup for dinner.

A growing child's brain needs healthy nutrition; consistent deprivation can negatively impact brain health and hold children back from easily creating a positive mood . . . and then there is little hope for cultivating inner confidence.

Your ability to provide for your child is likely much better than that of Tenzin's family. That's a good thing. But most of us Westerners get lazy and feed our children fast food and skimp on nutrition to make our lives easier, even though we "know better" about health and nutrition. There's nothing necessarily wrong with making your life easy—we all want simpler lives, but we also want our children to build strong immune systems, bones, and muscles. This happens primarily through providing our children nutritious foods, minerals, and vitamins on a consistent basis.

I also realize this isn't as easy as it sounds. My friend's son Nicholas, like so many children, is a picky eater. I've seen his father get creative by feeding him gummy vitamins, making protein or ice cream shakes, rewarding him for tasting new foods, and being diligent about ensuring that he gets what a growing child's brain needs, such as vitamins and minerals. Nicholas is also involved in the process of making dinner, and I often talk to him about how what we eat impacts our mood, strength, and abilities.

If you want to brush up on the essential vitamins a child needs to develop a healthy brain and body, read Nicola Graimes's book *Brain Food for Kids* or consult your local naturopath or physician.

Proper Hydration

Children also need to stay properly hydrated for good brain health and to keep their bodies in optimum condition. Water is deemed the largest element in the body, and it accounts for more than 60 percent of our body fluids. Making sure your children are drinking enough water is essential to optimizing their biology.

The amount of water every child needs varies based on their unique metabolism, environmental conditions, and sweat rate. The American Academy of Pediatrics suggests that American children don't drink enough water; the general recommendation for children remains similar to adults—between six and eight glasses of water (not just fluids) a day, with more in hot temperatures or when physical activity is involved.

In addition to water, providing children real fruit juice is another way to keep them properly nourished and hydrated. Dr. Sears, the well-known pediatrician, suggests being careful to give your child 100 percent real juice as opposed to products labeled as "punches," "beverages," and "juice cocktails," which are considered junk juice drinks. The aim is to provide your child the purest fruit juice possible.

Without healthy foods and vitamins, proper sleep, enough water, and physical activity, it is absolutely impossible for a child to develop their deepest sense of confidence.

Affection

Children need hugs like plants need water. It is absolutely vital for their healthy development that they feel safe, loved, and supported. His Holiness the Fourteenth Dalai Lama credits much of his positive mindset and outlook on life as beginning with the affection from his mother.

Providing your children a healthy dose of affection on a daily basis (or whenever you see them) is a powerful ingredient in helping them grow their self-confidence. It is your love and unconditional support that gives them the strength and power to love themselves in the same way.

Confidence Workout

Optimizing a child's biology goes beyond eating right, sleeping well, and being properly hydrated to something deeper: teaching your child not only to take excellent care of his physical body but to hold it in a confident manner. I believe it is true that one feels more confident by standing tall, dressing properly, and putting your best foot forward.

The activity below is geared for children who want to increase their sense of self-confidence especially as it relates to how they hold their physical body. I remember being a bit uncertain in elementary school, and I never sat up straight in my seat. This exercise might have changed all that. An added benefit is that you, the adult, get to read this to your child and see the benefits firsthand. Enjoy.

Exercise:
(To be read aloud by an adult)

Close your eyes.

Think of someone you see as confident. Maybe it's a teacher, friend, or parent who moves through the world standing tall and being exactly who they came here to be. It might even be a superhero like Spider-Man* or Iron Man*, too. Get a really good picture of him* in your mind. Use your imagination. Once you see him, pretend that you can step into his body and experience life the way he does. You walk the way he walks, standing tall and feeling strong in every step you take while being him.

Continue to imagine how it feels to be him, and experience that sense of strength in every movement. Do the things you usually do—things like getting ready for your day, putting on your clothes—but imagine doing it with a little more confidence, fearlessness, and feeling positively strong. You have access to this same power that your superhero has, and now you can draw upon this feeling anytime.

Before you open your eyes, I want you to know that this strength and power is inside of you at all times. You only need to remember your superhero strength inside of you and call upon it to feel strong in your daily life. You can do this whether you are walking the dog or trying something for the very first time—I believe in you, and now you believe in you, too.

Open your eyes whenever you are ready.

*(*Feel free to change for girls and substitute Xena the Warrior Princess or Hermione Granger from Harry Potter for female superheroes, and also change him to her, etc.)*

Studies have shown that by "going somewhere" in your mind, you also go to that place in your body. That is why visualizations are used with professional athletes—they can see themselves succeeding in their mind's eye. That is the same process here. You can help your child see his or her strength—so soon they'll personally experience it, too.

Stories of Strength

Simon Helberg, a leading American actor on the television series *The Big Bang Theory*, was a black belt in karate by age ten. As a five-year-old, he saw the hit movie *The Karate Kid* and became so completely inspired and interested in karate that he asked his parents straightaway for karate lessons, and they signed him up.

On the *Late Late Show with Craig Ferguson*, Simon said, "I took physical karate, but what I kept was mental karate"—meaning he became both physically and mentally strong. His karate classes kept him physically fit and optimized his brain health. Simon also gained a deeper sense of belief in himself, especially as he became a black belt; he achieved the highest level of mastery this sport provides by an extremely young age.

As a result of Simon's personal experience mastering karate, he began believing in himself more fully and thinking positively.

Implementing Block Two: Beliefs

Children are what they believe themselves to be. It is this truth that leads us to the second Building Block of Confidence—Beliefs. Guiding children to begin forming beliefs that lean toward confidence instead of doubt is the goal of this Block. After a child's body is healthy and his or her brain is working at its optimal level, the next step is to steer his or her mind toward creating self-confident thoughts.

Of course, some challenges will present themselves on this path to inner power. Classmates might tease your children; exams may not reflect their perfection back to them. A child's sense of inner confidence isn't built in one day but is done over time with repetition of consistent messages (both verbal and nonverbal) that gradually build inner strength.

Anchoring Confidence

Anchoring a child's sense of confidence in something deeper, like a story from a wisdom tradition or real-life experience, is helpful. Your child can hear the story from you repeatedly, or when alone he or she can recall it—that way the story will continue to inform him or her and strengthen an emerging sense of inner confidence.

Some wise teachings to anchor confidence include:

- **Precious Human Life.** Ancient Buddhist scholars like Shantideva taught in *A Guide to the Bodhisattva's Way of Life* that a precious human life is an incredibly rare gift, and when you have one, you have great potential and possibilities. This kind of teaching instills a sense of inner confidence in practitioners. When I was teaching children's programs, I also shared this wisdom with kids through children's books and reinforced it with coloring activities.

- **The Kingdom Within.** Christian leaders teach that the kingdom of heaven is within and that each person has the power to "move mountains" like Jesus did. The idea that within each of us is a divine spark from God (whether you call that Jesus, Source, Spirit, or another name) is a powerful notion to build a child's growing sense of confidence.

• **God Is with Me.** Ernest Holmes, founder of the Science of Mind teachings, explained, "I live in the faith that there is a Presence and Power greater than I am that nurtures and supports me in ways I could not even imagine. I know that this Presence is All-Knowing and All Power and is Always right where I am." By guiding children to believe they are never alone and that God is always near helps empower them.

More contemporary and less "religious" types of knowledge that can successfully anchor inner confidence are:

• **The Power Is Within You.** Louise Hay's popular book *The Power Is Within You* is a nondenominational explanation of how each of us has a power within us that can be used to live the life of our dreams. In the world of contemporary spirituality, there exist countless books for children of all ages to help you teach them how strong they are on the inside. One book for younger children is Wayne Dyer's *Incredible You!* which helps young kids embrace their power.

• **Greatness.** Wallace Wattles's book *The Science of Being Great* teaches that the greatness within the greatest people who ever lived (like Mother Teresa, George Washington, and Albert Einstein) is the same greatness within you and your child. You can also customize this teaching by drawing upon your son's or daughter's heroes and emphasize that greatness is within him or her, too.

When children become familiar with stories that empower their greatness and encourage their dreams, they learn how powerful they are right now. Again, the goal is to train their minds to repeatedly see themselves as powerful and to experience their power directly so they begin growing inner confidence through the habit of believing in themselves.

Power of Positive Thinking

Our thinking is what creates our life. Like me, you have probably had the experience of thinking of someone and boom—they are at your front step, calling you on the telephone, or sending you a text message. It is the power of our thinking that helps shape the invisible forces in the universe to create our life experience. I am not suggesting you raise your children in a "bubble" of idealistic thinking—but it is skillful to guide them to see the good (or God) in everything.

I attended a Catholic elementary school where I was motivated through fear. I distinctly remember Sister Mary telling me that if I didn't stop chewing my gum, I would go to "H—E—double hockey sticks," meaning "hell." I didn't find this experience did much to strengthen my positive-thinking muscle. Things are different today. I have found that children—by and large—are raised by parents and teachers who are doing what they can to strengthen children's sense of positivity and optimism.

I personally believe that the more you ground your child's emerging sense of confidence in a wisdom tradition, the easier it is for your child to think (the head) and feel (the heart) confident. Because I've anchored my belief system in a wisdom tradition, I find myself to be increasingly optimistic about my potential. (My personal wisdom tradition is Buddhism, but there are others you and your child might gravitate to.) Complementing my thinking with contemporary spiritual teachers of many traditions also allows me to claim my power in different ways on a daily basis.

Your tradition might be something spiritual but not religious. It might be going on weekly mindfulness walks together and listening to Abraham Hicks. I am not the person to tell you what you need to do—I just know from experience that every child that is nurtured consistently with insightful and empowering thoughts will begin thinking of himself or herself and the experience of life more positively.

Sam's Story

One uneventful Wednesday, Sam came home from school and started eating his usual snack of pretzels and orange juice. Everything was well in his fifth-grade world. His mother (and my friend), Cecelia, needed to speak to him that day and explain that he was wait-listed for a very popular charter school that he had his heart set on attending. And because she wanted to say "all the right things," Cecelia asked for me to come over, give her some suggestions, and lend her some support.

The good news is that Sam was amazingly okay with his mother's news. I mean, at first he looked crestfallen but after I spoke to him, he was more at peace. I told him:

Sam, there are no accidents. There is only God and good in every situation. I know sometimes we don't know why things happen, and that's okay. I also know that when we have our heart set on something, it is normal and healthy to feel sad when it doesn't work out. But please consider this: You now have many opportunities available to you to attend other magnet schools and private schools. This other school that you wind up going to may have your BFF (best friend forever), and through this turn of events you meet that person. You see, we never really know how life is going to work out. We must solely give it our best and do what is ours to do. Then we release it into the Universe knowing the perfect thing happens every time—that is the perfect thing to help us grow and expand our capacity to love.

After our discussion, Sam was a lot less stuck in thinking "Darn, this stinks" or "Boy, my mother messed up by applying late" to a more positive mindset of "This too shall pass" and "Maybe this is a good thing." The reality is that it is not what happens to us in life but how we learn to think about it that seals our fate.

As Cecelia and Sam together learn how to see the "good" in situations—even those that at first blush appear like problems—they will begin the habit of positive thinking. By no means am I suggesting that life is all rainbows and light, but after more than four decades of living I can honestly say that everything in my life has nudged me to grow and become a better version of myself.

The Voice of Parents

The voice of parents is the voice of gods,
for to their children they are heaven's lieutenants.

—Shakespeare

Your words are a powerful part of how your children begin thinking about themselves and ultimately, nurturing their sense of self-confidence. In my practice, I have found that parents who focus on "saying just the right thing" more often than not have an easier time raising inwardly confident kids. Your words shape your children's earliest view of themselves and have the capacity to empower their dreams. Here are some suggestions to help you do just that:

• **Have a list of ready-made confidence-building sayings.** When you are rushing around getting your kids to school, getting yourself to work, or cooking dinner, you can still offer honest and sincere praise to your child, even if you are "too busy" to think of something completely new in the moment. Some confidence building sayings might include:

✓ Great job on the spelling quiz! You worked hard and that effort paid off.

✓ Thank you, sweetheart. I appreciate how powerful you are inside—thanks for using your power to help me today.

✓ Wow. You are really learning how to do _____ well.

- **Learn to generate a sincere belief in your children.** When children think we doubt them, it can be devastating for them. So the more we can stay on target and focused on cultivating an honest, openhearted, and genuine appreciation and belief in our kids' potential and capabilities, the more they will internalize that and do the same for themselves.

  Another way of saying this is to get your doubts in check—don't pass uncertainty on to your children. Sometimes we doubt ourselves, and sometimes we doubt our children, and it takes a level of awareness and mindfulness to cease negative thoughts and replace them with more empowering ones. I've found Thich Nhat Hanh's *The Art of Power* inspiring and helpful on this topic; he describes the five spiritual powers: Mindfulness, Diligence, Faith, Concentration, and Insight.

- **Help your children see themselves succeed.** Sharing your empowering beliefs with your children is a good starting point. Then they need you to be their biggest advocates along the way, especially if they are experiencing challenges—poor grades, college rejection letters, a best friend moving away, or other disappointments that may be perceived as failures. This is where you as their parent can step in and give your children the big-picture view that everything in life is: a) a lesson, b) an opportunity for growth, and c) fodder for inner confidence.

Stories of Strength

Rachel, a British mother of two, reads to her children every evening as part of their bedtime ritual. Rachel says, "I believe these stories are the simplest and most profound way to teach my kids to believe in themselves more and more each day." She selects books with empowering stories and uses her own imagination to spark her children's inner strength.

Drawing on her cultural heritage, Rachel reads A. A. Milne's *Winnie the Pooh* books and Beatrix Potter's *Peter Rabbit* series. (For instance, Potter's *Jeremy Fisher* teaches kids about the "right amount" of confidence: Jeremy the frog almost gets eaten by a fish because of overconfidence.)

Regardless of the method used to impart the lesson, the goal is to help your children experience their power and begin thinking confidently about their capabilities.

Implementing Block Three: Emotions

Emotions are energy in motion. They supercharge thoughts and amplify confidence. It is the confident feeling that children love to experience, and they can learn to create the thoughts that produce that feeling.

The Confident Feeling

Growing up as a rather insecure child, I found feeling confident next to impossible. My family of origin, like so many, was rather dysfunctional. I was a latchkey kid by the time I was nine, letting myself into the house after school, getting my own snacks, and then relaxing in front of the television. My parents weren't bad people, just busy with their own full-time jobs and health challenges.

Looking back, the Five Building Blocks of Confidence were never in play. I didn't eat well, get physical activity, healthy hugs, or begin thinking positively. My family was concerned about surviving versus thriving. So the idea of feeling self-confident was a completely foreign idea to me. I grew up really wondering how other children could feel so good about themselves. Now I know they had healthier role models, but they also had these Blocks animated in their lives.

I share my story not because I am special or have had any unique experiences, but because I understand the power of the Five Building Blocks of Confidence both personally and professionally.

One of my colleagues, Ava, did me a favor and asked her two children what they thought confidence means and feels like. These are their responses:

- Rose, age eleven, said that confidence is "to have faith in yourself, to know you can do something." Ava then asked Rose when she felt confident, and her response was "Hmm. When I make good test scores. Or when I've done something before and know how to do it." Rose's response is the common answer from children pointing to outer confidence. The feeling that they have mastered something and can do it again with ease.

- Marcus, age four, is Ava's second child. He is at a different stage of development especially as it pertains to confidence. She asked him what confidence is, and he said "I don't know," which is not surprising. Ava explained confidence and then asked Marcus if he ever feels confident. He replied, "I am good at coloring. I am good at drawing. I am good at gingerbread houses. I am good at blowing out candles."

Both Rose and Marcus understand outer confidence. This is a

good thing because it can be used as a stepping-stone toward inner confidence. Since I know Ava and I have observed her children get proper exercise, eat healthfully (most of the time), and (for the most part) get adequate sleep, I see Block One: Biology coming to life.

The challenge for Ava and her husband, Brian, now is to be consistent role models of inner confidence and guide their children to think in this way, too. Rose, who is now in middle school and full of hormonal responses, is often swayed by little situations, thinking they are the "worst ever" and needing her parents' guidance to help her think more positively about things—from flunking a test to being teased on the bus. Marcus (who is in preschool) is just beginning to form a perception of the world as friendly and supportive, largely due to his parent's guidance.

Inner and Outer Confidence

Going from outer to inner confidence is the work of every parent and child. None of us escapes this process if we are on Planet Earth. You and your children have the sacred work of expanding into the fullest versions of yourselves and learning how to have faith in yourselves . . . and that can lead to inner confidence.

You can see the difference in how children begin thinking when guided toward inner confidence. Nearly all children begin thinking thoughts of outer confidence and producing the correlated feelings. That's perfectly normal. But with guidance and a little extra instruction, your son or daughter can also begin thinking more inwardly confident thoughts. Children want to believe that within them is everything they need to be happy and successful—they are merely waiting for someone to confirm it with them.

How Inner Confidence and Outer Confidence Feel

Outer Confidence:

A sense of strength based on outer circumstances, whether it's getting a new haircut, kicking a winning goal, or receiving a straight-A report card. Once these "outer" things have been accomplished, both adults and children feel good about themselves (self-esteem) and confident in their abilities (outer confidence). This feeling is a surface type of faith in one's self that is easily shaken.

Inner Confidence:

A sense of strength based on inner knowledge, and the wisdom that within you exists all the power, capability, and potential to succeed. It feels like inner peace, calmness, and self-trust. Your inner voice says, "No matter what happens, I feel good [about my capabilities]. I trust myself. I know that I can succeed." There are no external conditions that need to be met to feel good inside and think confident thoughts.

Some things that have helped me generate the feeling, understanding, and experience of inner confidence include:

- Seeing myself succeed
- Being around people who possess inner confidence
- Studying it (for example, audio recordings like Pema Chodron's *Unconditional Confidence,* or reading books like *Morning Sunshine: How to Radiate Confidence and Feel It, Too* by CNN anchor Robin Meade)
- Speaking to myself confidently
- Having others speak to me confidently

Each of these experiences can accelerate inner confidence. My suggestion is to study inner confidence on a consistent basis, put these ideas into play, and watch your life transform.

Years ago, I traveled to South Asia by myself, which both required and cultivated my inner confidence. First, I had to believe that within me existed the power and capability to successfully complete the trip. Second, I succeeded at "risky" activities like traveling alone, riding on the top of a bus, eating foreign foods, teaching in a new language, showering out of buckets, and surviving without heat in the middle of the winter. Once I saw myself tackle each challenge, I developed a deeper level of intelligent faith in myself.

Children need to also experience a sense of their inner strength. Alfonso, a ten-year-old client of mine, got to travel alone for the first time this year. He told me, "It made me feel like I could do anything. I loved it!" Again, it is through Alfonso's direct experience with flying alone that he can feel more confident in doing it again—or alternatively, trying new experiences and succeeding at those.

Confidence Workout

You cannot bolster your sense of inner confidence without feeling it. Similar to learning how to think confident thoughts, you and your child need to get into the habit of feeling confident feelings through daily practices and empowering habits.

Some of my favorite exercises are inspired by the work of Esther and Jerry Hicks in their book *Ask and It Is Given.* The following are three new exercises I've created to discover how to feel good and manifest your desires.

Exercise One: With your son or daughter, play this "Fill In the Blank" game to build outer and inner confidence. Ask him or her to complete this line:

I am so happy and grateful now that I feel confident about_____.

The goal is to encourage your child to feel confident about tasks he or she is mastering today. Some suggestions are:

Reading	Making a campfire (with help)	Making journals
Shooting darts		Using watercolors
Winning at Voxatron	Meditation	Making homemade holiday cards
Doing cartwheels	Bathing the dog	
Singing	Helping others	Playing soccer
Saying prayers	Learning Spanish	Pitching a tent
Setting the table	Playing "Twinkle, Twinkle Little Star" on the piano	Filling the birdfeeder
Raising money for charity		Making my own lunch
		Practicing Yoga

It's important to be as specific as possible, so if your daughter feels talented at Uno, encourage her to say that.

Exercise Two: You'll lead your child in this "Positive Things" game to help build his or her feelings of optimism and healthy self-regard.

Take out a piece of paper and encourage your child to draw, use words, or somehow capture all the positive things around him or her. If drawing or writing seem too academic, he or she can just list them verbally. But I would start by saying:

Today, we are going to learn how to *see* the positive things in our life. It's a fun game and let me start. I see the sun shining, hear the birds chirping, feel blessed to have electricity, heat, and a Pug named Shiva. I love my work because it helps me express my creativity, meet so many great people, and travel to neat places. I love your dad because he works hard for the family, tells many funny jokes, and is a great cook. I love you because you are you—you don't need to do anything to make me love you. You are lovable just as you are.

This is a verbal rampage of positivity and can easily turn into a coloring project. Children don't always put crayons, pencils, and coloring markers to paper as much as previous generations, so I often suggest they do this. It helps them grow their hand-eye coordination while providing a healthy outlet for their creativity, and, in this instance, teaches them how to look for the positive things in life.

Exercise Three: I call this the "Pizza Slice" game. The goal is to help your child feel more confident about himself or herself.

Take out a piece of white paper for yourself and one for your child. Lead him or her to draw a circle and divide it up into eight slices—like a pizza pie. In each slice of your own paper, each of you draws something that you feel REALLY, REALLY good about yourself. This helps build confidence.

A child client of mine, Anna, divided her paper into eight slices and drew: Her climbing wall abilities; her ability to make short books; her ability to put together the Star Wars Lego set; and the way she swings on the playground swings to start. These four things are big things in her life and highlight her natural intelligences—linguistic (book covers, books), analytical (putting together sets), and physical (climbing wall, outdoor play)—which helped her feel really good about her abilities. She then continued filling in the other four slices of the pie.

Anna literally beamed from this project, and said "Thanks, I am going to hang this up in my room today!" Repeating simple exercises like this will encourage a child to embrace and claim his or her confidence.

Stories of Strength

Gisela, an Argentinian mother I interviewed, was emphatic about the importance of helping children feel great. "Reward children with love," she said, "and you will see their spirits soar and confidence get created."

Luis, her seven-year-old son, is obsessed with football—or soccer, as we call it. He practices every day, and on weekends, Gisela attends his tournaments. At the games, she likes to hold up homemade banners that read "GO LUIS!" Last weekend, Luis told his mom that those signs made him feel that he could really do it.

Becoming your children's biggest advocate and helping them feel confident that whatever they put their mind to they can do, be, or have is parenting at its best.

Implementing Block Four: Social

After your child's body and brain have been optimized (Block One), thoughts steered toward creating inner confidence (Block Two), and feelings of inner strength sparked (Block Three), it is time to move on to Block Four—Social. In this Block, the importance of consistent feedback is underscored as a key component in reinforcing a child's sense of confidence.

Are the other people in your child's life supporting his or her development of inner confidence? Is Lucy attending after-school classes where the teacher praises her inner capabilities? Does Junior receive weekly kudos for a job well-done at Boy Scouts? The more children receive *outer feedback* confirming their inner strength, the quicker *inner confidence* builds.

Another key piece of this Block is how children talk to themselves. Like all of us, children need to master the skill of positive self-talk by repeatedly say affirming, confidence-building things to themselves. The sooner kids become adept at positive thinking and self-talk (inner feedback), the easier confidence is created.

Confidence Feedback Loops

In the last chapter, I introduced the term "confidence feedback loop" to capture the process of providing a child consistent circles of feedback. This feedback is either *outer*—for example, from parents, report cards, and competitions—or *inner*, like self-talk and feelings. Parents have the golden opportunity to place outer confidence feedback loops into their children's lives and also guide them to create high-quality inner loops. Both types of loops can foster inner confidence.

Some practical suggestions to begin this process include:

- **Review your child's current activities**. Do they consistently provide positive feedback and affirm your child's inner power and capabilities? Are these activities held regularly?
- **Think about your child's daily schedule.** Do you read to him or her daily, or say daily affirmations together? Can you find five minutes in the day to build your child's repertoire of positive self-talk? (The car ride to school counts. Plus, they are captive then—just perfect!)
- **Keep your eyes open.** Are you familiar with local confidence-building activities? By local, I mean extracurricular programs in your community like kid's meditation classes and archery or other activities that nurture your child's growing sense of outer and inner confidence.

In the Social Block, parents have an opportunity to mindfully look at a child's *outer feedback loops* (school, activities, friends, teachers, and interests) and assess if they are empowering a child's inner sense of strength. My colleague, Maria, did just that and decided to cut out "filler activities" that just kept her kids busy and to focus predominantly on things that build their self-esteem, confidence, and character—while having fun, too.

Some loops may build a child's outer confidence—like mastering a sport—and then, in turn, the accomplishment from that activity can lead him or her on the path toward inner confidence. However, if you want to focus on *creating* inner confidence, those outer confidence loops need to be complemented by inner confidence loops, either those you suggest to your child that focuses him or her inward or by another activity. Some inner-focused activities are listed below. What makes them inner focused is the emphasis on the "inner" changes taking place in children like calmness, energy movement, prayer, and mindfulness so kids can be witness and welcome the power inside of them.

- Kid's Yoga, tai chi, and karate
- Meditation
- Spiritual classes
- Music lessons (especially those that focus on inner abilities)
- Mindfulness walks

Of course, any class or activity is only as good as the teacher. The class isn't as important as finding the right teacher (mentor, guide) to lead your child to a place of deeper belief in his or her power within.

Children who receive consistent confidence-building feedback in outer loops will also naturally begin speaking to themselves positively. If children repeatedly hear that they are highly capable and talented, then they will believe it and speak to themselves in the same way. This is an inner confidence feedback loop. Because the loop strengthens their belief in their inner capability to succeed, it is a confidence feedback loop. This is different than merely feeling good about one's self, which is self-esteem.

The challenge is when children receive mixed messages, which they often do. Jeff's teacher Mrs. Smith tells him, "You are my star student!" But when Jeff goes home, his grandmother exclaims, "Jeff, your homework is messy and full of mistakes!" What will Jeff think? Children are merely seeking to navigate their worlds and feel good about themselves. But if Jeff has cultivated a sense of inner confidence, his grandmother's words won't shake his confidence—his faith will be grounded in something deeper, something within him instead of something "out there."

One way for a child to strengthen his or her core self and inner confidence is to use confidence-building sayings when conflicting messages present themselves—as they always do. One of my child clients, Jackie, repeatedly says, "I am happy, strong, and perfect right now. All is well." Sometimes she struggles with her parent's recent divorce and needs to be reminded that she can create her every moment—it is up to her to decide if her day is a happy day, and her daily repetition of this mantra creates an inner confidence feedback loop.

Here are some other inner confidence feedback loops:

• **Mirror Exercises.** Children look in the mirror every day for one minute and acknowledge positive things about themselves: "I am pretty"; "I am smart"; "I can tie my shoelaces now"; "I love my dog, Fluffy," etc. These may seem like "outer" loops, but since your child is looking in her own eyes, this allows her to internalize these thoughts and begin speaking to herself in a more positive way.

- **Songs.** Music is a very effective way to build self-confidence in a playful and often physically active way. Encourage children to find songs that empower them—and encourage them to dance, too! David Pomeranz's "It's in Every One of Us" helps children feel powerful from the inside out.

- **Prayer Pose.** My colleague, Aimee, spends between three and five minutes in prayer pose every morning with her daughter Anne. This is a fairly simple yoga pose that helps you turn inward, and along with this physical reminder, Aimee says: "We are both strong inside. Today is a happy day, and everything goes our way!" This helps Anne and Aimee connect to their power in a simple way, and since they are affirming their inner strength, it is an inner confidence feedback loop.

You're parenting effectively when you purposefully focus on building a child's inner strength through giving him or her direct experiences of seeing his or her power within on a regular basis.

Confidence Workout

One of my most popular projects for children is a "dream journal," where they can identify, record, and express their innermost wishes and dreams. Dreams might include becoming an elementary school teacher, an Olympic gymnast, or a spaceship mechanic. Or they could include growing a garden this summer, buying a new bicycle, making a new friend, or traveling to Paris, France, someday. The magic of this project is that it gives children a safe space to express their dreams and strengthen their belief in themselves—that they can do, be, or have anything their heart desires.

Exercise:
(Adult supervision needed)

Materials: • Journal full of blank pages (no lines), either
store-bought or homemade
• Scissors, glue, stickers, tape, magazines,
photos, and favorite things
• Crayons, markers, colored pencils,
and other writing implements
• Reference books (or Internet)
to look things up

In this exercise, adult supervision is suggested for young children because scissors will be used—and also to encourage a child to freely dream his or her biggest dream.

(To be read aloud by an adult)

A "dream journal" is a place where you can identify and encourage your dreams. If Kayla wants to become a veterinarian, she may cut out images of dogs, cats, birds, and doctors from magazines and paste these into the journal along with writing "Kayla, the Vet: Open for Business!" Or perhaps Kayla wants to visit Paris, France, someday; she could draw the Eiffel Tower and herself on top of it smiling. You get the idea.

My hope is that this journal becomes your special place to put your unique dreams and make you feel that it's all possible—because it is!

You can also add to this journal anytime, take things out and look at it for inspiration, or to get that special *umph* feeling that you can do it and the world will support you in making your dreams come true. Let's get started.

Encouraging their dreams and recording confidence-building messages helps children stay connected to the truth of their inner power. Some of my child clients have created amazing journals—pasting in photos of themselves kicking a winning goal or receiving a certificate of accomplishment, drawing their big dreams as already done, taping in the lyrics of their favorite song, writing their own message to the Universe, or making their own childhood "bucket list" of things they want to do.

Children who look with positive expectation at their dream journals over and over again are putting a positive inner "confidence feedback loop" into place—and this alone strengthens their growing sense of confidence.

Stories of Strength

Agape is a small orphanage in South Africa with an amazing children's choir. All thirty-plus children are AIDS orphans; their saving grace is a community that provides them food, shelter, clothes, love, and a place to sing. The power of this community is beyond the sum of its people, and it is a place that teaches these kids they are powerful, capable, and valuable today.

Years ago, I had the privilege of meeting the children of Agape's orphanage, and I was most impressed. These children felt blessed, loved, and supported in bringing their unique choir to the world. Gogo, the headmaster of Agape, had succeeded at setting up consistent outer feedback loops that reinforced to these children that they are unconditionally loved, immeasurably talented, and surely capable of succeeding at whatever they wished. Some of those daily loops were empowering songs, community prayer, and affirmations in the morning.

The film *We Are Together* brings their story to life. Through the course of promoting this film, these children also raised over £250,000 or about

$358, 000 to help orphans throughout South Africa. This is the power of strengthening children: in turn, they will also strengthen others.

Implementing Block Five: Spiritual

Connecting children to their core selves and spiritual essence will strengthen their sense of inner confidence. This Block is the icing on the cake: A child must have a healthy brain, then begin thinking confident thoughts and feeling those feelings before confidence can be strengthened through feedback and expanded through a spiritual connection. In this fifth and final Block, children's confidence is cemented by a connection to "something greater."

This "something greater" comes in all sorts of forms. It may be a traditionally religious figure, like Jesus; metaphysical, like Spirit; or earthy and grounding, like nature. When children believe in a greater power and see it around their lives—in waterfalls, rainbows, and chirping birds—they begin connecting to infinite intelligence. As children are guided to "see" this same power, intelligence, and energy within them, the spiritual Block comes alive.

The Spiritual Connection

Children come to personally experience their spiritual essence and inner power in many different ways. One way isn't necessarily better than another—each has its wisdom and ability to strengthen a child's sense of inner confidence. The secret to accelerating children's connection to their "something greater" is in finding what lights them up and connecting them to it.

Some common ways children come to personally experience their great spirit are through:

- **Nature**—Hiking, climbing, camping, swimming, spending time at the beach or in the mountains, gardening, and walking
- **Music**—Playing an instrument like the drums or listening to your favorite musician on a great sound system
- **Movement**—Being in a class (like ballet, yoga, or karate) or some physical activity that requires flexibility, focus, and inner strength
- **Visual Arts**—Drawing with a pencil, painting a mural, building a tree house, or building model airplanes
- **Analytical**—Looking in a telescope, seeing a laser light show, and getting lost in mathematical equations of the infinite
- **Spiritual Practice**—Saying prayers, going to services, listening to teachers, or helping others

How you help your child know the expansiveness of his or her spirit—whether it is seeing a double rainbow, playing African drums, learning a new dance step, or bowing in front of a religious image—doesn't matter. The point is that your child has the opportunity to get into a creative and inspired state and directly experience his or her limitless power.

Since I live near the Blue Ridge Mountains in North Carolina, I am fortunate that I get to visit some of the most beautiful waterfalls in this area. They are large and majestic, and you can explore them all year long. They inspire me. So last fall, I took my friend's son, Nicholas, on a hike and he absolutely loved being in the waterfall. Afterward, he told me it made him "feel happy to be alive." I couldn't have said it better.

Confidence Workout

Children who know that their spirit is powerful and that this force is connected to "something greater" are well-positioned to build inner confidence. A colleague of mine, Josephine, guides her two daughters to see and use this power in a nightly *loving-kindness meditation* that sends positive energy to other people. When children see that they can do this meditation any time, they begin to believe more firmly that this power exists within them.

Exercise:

(To be read aloud by an adult)

Tonight, let's do something new. It's called a loving-kindness meditation.

We are going to send love—pure positive energy from inside you—to others in the world. It is this energy and pure force of unconditional positive wishes to people that lifts their spirits, heals their minds, and changes their lives so they get happier.

Let's start now. Close your eyes or leave them open, whatever you prefer. Begin thinking of something you love, and really feel the feeling of love that goes with it. It may be your pet, best friend, stuffed animal, or sport you love playing. Do you feel it?

[Wait for a Yes.]

Take this feeling of love and let's send it to the people we know: Send it to your friends [name them], teachers [continue naming throughout], family members, cousins, distant relatives, neighbors, and anyone else who comes to mind [keep naming them].

Now, send this feeling of love that heals to those people you don't know on Planet Earth. The kids in other countries who have tummy aches, are hungry or sick, need clothes, want to go to better schools, and want to have more happy days playing in the sun.

Let's also send love to all the animals on Planet Earth, like dolphins, birds, seagulls, puppy dogs, cats, elephants, tigers, tarantulas, and more. [Have child name them.]

Thank you for using that great spiritual power inside of you to heal, change, and make the world a happier place. You are so powerful!

Stories of Strength

Dolma, a new mother in New Delhi, India, arrived home from the hospital with her newborn. Her home was in Maju Ka Tilla, a Tibetan refugee resettlement community. The first place she took her new baby boy upon arrival home was to the family altar. Introducing the newest family member to their spiritual life and traditions, which included making offerings, reciting prayers and a deep reverence for His Holiness the Dalai Lama and the Buddha, was the foremost thing on her mind.

In her own words, Dolma explained, "Dhargye's spiritual life is the most important. My role as his mother is to love him and put him on the right spiritual path." Her culture of Tibetan Buddhism is also infused with spirituality, whether it is starting her day saying the sacred mantra of "Ohm Mani Padme Hung" or attending the teachings of their spiritual leader, His Holiness the Fourteenth Dalai Lama.

Within the context of Buddhism, Dolma's son will grow up learning that within him is the power or "seed" of enlightenment. Such an idea helps a child believe that he has the strength to overcome any obstacles, especially those that prevent him from being genuinely happy.

Bringing It All Together

The Five Building Blocks of Confidence is a powerful system that clarifies how confidence is created. Each Block is an essential ingredient to the recipe of inner confidence. When all five Blocks are working optimally, with wisdom and love, it is impossible for self-confidence *not* to flourish.

Experience shows us that if we leave any of the Blocks out, the efficacy of the Building Blocks diminishes. These Blocks are sequential, with one building upon the next. Inner confidence isn't even possible without Block One, a child's healthy biology, and Block Two, a mind focused on creating confident thoughts. If a child forgets to feel confidence (Block Three), then his confidence lessens; if this baseline sense of confidence isn't supported by others, then it begins to shrink (Block Four), and if a child never connects with "something greater," the depth of confidence isn't expanded to its capacity (Block Five).

Each Block plays a very synergistic and progressive role in the creation of outer and inner confidence. At the same time, the reality is that all of these Blocks are happening all the time. A child is eating before soccer practice (Block One), then he attends his soccer team meeting, where the children are pumped up with confidence (Block Two and Block Three), and get really positive feedback (Block Four) before heading out to the amazingly beautiful field (Block Five).

If we mindfully review each Block, seek to optimize it, and have fun during the process, inner confidence will come to our children sooner and easier.

Of course, this requires that you and I stay focused on the goal. The goal is to create inner confidence in our children: a belief in your child's heart-mind that they have the power within them to succeed no matter what!

5

The Connection Between Confidence and Happiness

Happiness must develop within ourselves; nobody can give it to us. Its ultimate source is tranquility or peace of mind. It doesn't depend on external factors. It doesn't matter if we lack good facilities, a good education or a successful life, as long as we have inner confidence.

—His Holiness the Fourteenth Dalai Lama

So far, we've focused primarily on inner confidence and how to nurture this internal quality through the Five Building Blocks of Confidence. The development of inner confidence is a prerequisite for so many positive experiences that it is worth understanding what it is and how to bring it to life through the Building Blocks. Now we get to place it in the larger context of what everyone is looking for—happiness.

Within this chapter, I share specifically the connection between inner confidence and lasting happiness. In my travels around the globe meeting parents and teachers from all sorts of cultural, socio-economic, and educational backgrounds, I've found the one thing that ties everyone together is the deep wish beating in their hearts to raise happy children. It is for that reason I decided to write this book with the majority of it focused on inner confidence.

Once you "get" why inner confidence is the foundation for this deeper type of unshakeable happiness, it makes perfect sense to start there. If we started anywhere else, it would be like building a house starting with the second floor: You just can't do it. You must begin by laying the foundation, building a first floor, and continuing from there. One step follows the other on this path toward nurturing genuine happiness in your child.

Along with making the connection between confidence and happiness crystal clear, I also want to share with you what happiness means from an Eastern perspective. This is quite different from what most of us deem happiness to be in our fast paced world . . . so my suggestion is to consider these ideas with an open mind, and if you feel so compelled, explore them further. I promise the only thing you have to lose is your unhappiness.

I also share "Three Ways to Lasting Happiness for Kids" at the end of this chapter so that as you continue to nurture your child's inner confidence, you can keep your eyes peeled for happiness opportunities, too.

The Happiness Boom

Over the past few years, I have observed a surge in products that claim to make you happier. Whether it is buying a new Porsche (money can buy happiness), shampoo (being more attractive can buy happiness), or heading to your favorite website like Parents.com, which claims to give you "Healthy Kids, Happy Families," this happiness thing is being sold everywhere.

But what is really being sold? Let's look at an example. Say later today, I go out and buy a new Porsche Boxster—that certainly will make me happy. I am going to enjoy the wind in my hair, the speed it can go (okay, I'll leave all kids at home!) and just luxuriating in the beauty of this vehicle. It feels like a happy move. But eventually, the car will get a scratch or no longer run, and my sense of happiness will end.

This is *fleeting happiness*. Most advertisers are capitalizing on the "fast food" mentality of our culture that wants things now. They are selling a temporary sense of joy. Of course, buying and enjoying a new car isn't bad; the point is that it's an external possession. Anything "out there" is only going to give you a fleeting sense of happiness. Turning outward to find happiness in things like cars, spouses, houses, and gadgets will always lead to disappointment.

True happiness can be so much deeper; unlike the car that breaks down, the job that ends, the house that floods, true happiness is lasting and unshakable. Many people have never even experienced this type of happiness because they're too obsessed with gaining fleeting happiness through possessions. True or *lasting happiness* comes from turning inward and creating a place of peace within. And with practice, you can also guide your child to develop that same peace that transcends the problems of everyday living.

Fleeting Happiness	A temporary sense of joy: Your son wants an ice-cream cone, and he is so excited when you buy him a double scoop of chocolate with sprinkles. But once it's gone, so is his temporary sense of happiness.

Lasting Happiness   A permanent sense of calm abiding and peace. A great example is Hara, a nine-year-old who lived through the Japanese Tsunami of 2011. This was a devastating experience for her parents, community, and friends. But she'd been taught her entire life to "go within" to feel happy, and that everything "out there" wasn't a source of happiness. So despite her school being shut down and her best friend moving away, Hara stayed calm and mostly content inside.

Cultivating lasting happiness is our life's work. Hara is on the path of developing this deeper sense of happiness, and despite this tragic experience, she showed indications that it is growing within her.

Kids' happiness begins as fleeting happiness. With guidance, it can develop into this deeper form of happiness—lasting happiness. Kids touch this infinite place of inner calmness especially after learning how to meditate, or when they're immersed in creative projects and pursuits they love. It is here where they are in "the flow" and connected to all there is. I believe that children who come to know this place within and learn how to make it "more real" than everything in the outer world are well positioned to create this deeper happiness that feels like inner peace.

The How of Happiness

Most people are about as happy
as they make their minds up to be.

—Abraham Lincoln

One of the great things about where I am now in my life is that I no longer need to get the perfect house, spouse, car, or wardrobe to feel that okay—I can be happy now. My decision to be happy is merely created by something inside of me because I realize it's a choice (as well as function of my optimized biology). My happiness is also a result of my ability to connect with happiness teachers and change my mind about when I can be happy.

Most Western adults I meet are playing that subconscious game most of us have played—it goes like this: I will be happy when _____ (fill in the blank). How did you fill in the blank? Perhaps, it was "when my spouse takes the garbage out without me asking" or "when my daughter actually listens and picks up her library books from all over the floor." The blank is the problem. The blank never goes away. Searching for the blank is how fleeting happiness is created; we want things on the outside to make us happier.

The deeper type of happiness that I describe above has nothing to do with the blank. It is about learning how to create this place inside of us that is happy—period, end of story.

Happiness like this can happen for any parent and child. That's the great news. It doesn't happen overnight, though. That's the rub. Some things in life (I promise) are worth creating and putting the time into, because what you reap will be far greater than the seeds you planted. This is the case for lasting happiness. Think about being peaceful when you are stuck in traffic, waiting in the ridiculous line in the supermarket, or when you get an outrageous mobile phone bill—wouldn't that feel great? With lasting happiness, you learn how to not get "hooked" by the things that make you unhappy over and over again.

Some more good news is that we don't need to start from scratch. Happiness teachers throughout time have left breadcrumbs so we

can find our way—and we can help our children create that place
inside, too.

Breadcrumbs on the Way

*Only by coming back to ourselves and purifying our minds
can we experience true, lasting happiness and the kind of
power that can't be corrupted.*

—Thich Nhat Hanh, Vietnamese Zen Teacher

Our Western world has produced excellent scientific studies
evidencing that happier kids' feel physically stronger, eat healthier
overall, connect to spirituality, and have multiple friends who make
them feel valued. All of these are valuable points that lead us to what
happiness is and how to generate it in our youngest generation. The
problem in my mind is that we continue to raise children focused
upon fleeting happiness when there is so much more. . . .

Happiness in children can go deeper. They can now learn how to
touch this place inside of them that is peaceful and goes beyond our
common understanding of happiness—they can begin to seed lasting happiness.

So here is where I bring in Buddhist philosophy that best explains
the ideas of what lasting happiness really is, which I share because it
is the most compelling to me. It combines the cultivation of wisdom
(knowledge with experience) along with personal experience or
practice in learning how to increase positive emotions like compassion while reducing pesky ones like anger that really show up unan-
nounced as well as with great force.

In his book, *Live in a Better Way*, His Holiness the Fourteenth Dalai Lama tells how:

> From birth we have the right to be happy, and lasting happiness must develop within ourselves; nobody can give it to us and no external factor can be responsible for it. It must be achieved through our own inner development.

Becoming happy no matter what is therefore an inside job. Inside of us—mentally and emotionally—we create a space where positive emotions like love, compassion, and gratitude have been increased, while negative emotions like anger, hatred, fear, and jealousy have been decreased. It leaves us with a mind that is clear, luminous, and unobstructed by the sway of negative emotions. This type of mind has great power, and when connected with wisdom, it has the capacity to develop intelligent worldviews free of ignorance and common misperceptions.

For example, one common misperception many of us have is that our lives and experiences are permanent. Sadness is the perfect case in point. I find so many children get "stuck" in sadness because they don't realize that it will go away like a cloud floating along (they also misidentify themselves as being that cloud). Children need guidance that they are not what they are feeling. Whatever emotion they are having (sadness, joy, excitement, disappointment, anger, jealousy) is temporary and will pass. Without guidance, children automatically assume that the sadness they have is going to last forever. This is a very dangerous (and depressing) assumption. Having been both a student and teacher of Buddhism, I have had the good fortune of understanding the "true nature" of our mind as being like a blue sky—clear and bright and helping kids get it, too.

Creating this clear mind doesn't require that you become Buddhist. It solely requires that you commit to remove the obstacles to clarity, and help guide your child to do the same (perhaps by enrolling him or her in an emotionally intelligent school). And like inner confidence, the creation of a clear mind is a process—two steps forward, one step back, three steps forward, and so on. But I promise you that as your mind lets go of any illusions, false thoughts, and the baggage you've carried for years, your mind will become more and more like a clear blue, bright sky—its true nature. Sadness will still come up because that's the nature of life, but you won't get stuck in it—you'll be clear what it is and how to guide yourself, as well as your child, healthfully through it.

Connecting Confidence to Happiness

The one who has conquered himself
is a far greater hero than he who
has defeated a thousand times a thousand men.

—Buddha

Creating lasting happiness is about conquering one's self . . . the self that is constantly seeking to find immediate satisfaction in food, drink, music, and movies. I am by no means saying you should give up worldly pleasures since I love many of those things, too. The point is that you want to be free of seeking happiness in anything "out there" and be able to find peace and contentment within you. Putting this simple statement into practice takes a whole lot of inner confidence.

Lasting happiness is like an Olympic gold medal: It's something that you aim for and with practice can achieve in this lifetime. It is a state of mind free from disturbances, and it allows you to be wherever you are with a sense of peace.

Remember a time when you were really angry. I mean really, really angry. Someone said something to you or did something you saw as wrong. How did you feel? What did you do?

Earlier in my life, I would let my anger "take over." I can recall once kicking a hole in my wall. I was just so pissed off about something I now can't even remember—the point is that to tame the inner beast of anger and other destructive emotions, it takes a super-strong sense of self (the positive side of self) and great inner confidence. You need to believe that within you is the "capability" to create this place of peace—a place that begins catching your negative emotions, befriends them, holds them close, and applies antidotes to them so they reduce in force. I no longer kick holes in the wall, but I certainly will catch myself getting frustrated sometimes if I think someone is driving too slowly (oh my gosh). But the good news is that I actively do things to help me feel calmer, more peaceful, and yes—happier—day by day.

Children take our lead on happiness, just like they do with other examples we set. They learn whether happiness comes from the new toy or from something deeper. Of course, I want your child to be surrounded with all the things he or she loves—the stuffed SpongeBob, guinea pig named Pete, favorite plush beanbag chair, and crayons galore. I am solely suggesting you consciously point your children inward when they are looking to feel happiness and not "get caught" in the trap of thinking happiness is out there when you (fill in the blank).

Alex's Story

One of my child clients, ten-year-old Alex, learned how to better navigate his anger, reduce his knee-jerk reactions, and find more positive feeling thoughts. At age seven, Alex was put into the social services system after his parents died in a car accident. Although his sadness, disappointment, frustration, and anger were all justified responses to his past, his guardian Lisa realized that his angry outbursts were not making the situation better. This is how and why Alex became one of my clients.

After six months of weekly sessions, Alex had a breakthrough. He began to respond differently to situations that made him "mad." Instead of raising his voice or throwing things, Alex took up guitar and began going to karate lessons to "get out" all of his pent-up energy. Anger is merely energy in motion that needs a healthy outlet, and if Alex didn't have one, it became a problem.

The other piece of the anger puzzle is that Alex and Lisa learned how to apply patience, which is an antidote to anger. They learned to be patient when angry and to let this emotion come up and pass instead of "acting it out" immediately and having a big fight. This takes practice. It also takes a whole lot of inner confidence to believe that within you exists the power and strength to reduce that pesky emotion of anger.

But with practice, every parent and child can learn how to a) identify negative emotions like anger before they become problematic, b) apply antidotes to lessen them, and c) put positive emotions like patience in their place.

Confidence Comes Before Happiness

When I say confidence comes before happiness, I am talking about lasting happiness. Your children can experience fleeting happiness even if they are completely insecure about their capabilities. This type of temporary happiness only requires that you chase after something that will in that moment make you feel uplifted. For example, I know that nearly every child loves a huge basket of Halloween candy.

My close friends' son Nicholas loves Halloween, and he feels absolutely fantastic when he has his huge basket of candy. But when that candy is gone, he wants more; this "endless wanting" is part of unhappiness. It's the feeling within you that you can't be content with what you have but really must get *more* to be happy—in this case, more candy. I know this is a simple example, but it is applicable to most situations.

Instead of focusing on the candy (or the lack of it), you can plant more lasting seeds of happiness. Perhaps your family can sit around the table and each member give thanks to the people who helped make Halloween possible: candy factory workers, truck drivers, supermarket clerks, neighbors, costume designers, face painting companies, big orange Halloween basket makers, and the inventors of your favorite candies like Tootsie Rolls and SweeTarts. This simple exercise helps refocus your child away from only looking outside of himself or herself to developing his or her inner life.

Such inner development may include a practice of gratitude, generosity, compassion, love, forgiveness, honesty, patience, and perseverance. It is these inner qualities that help foster happiness inside and reduce negative emotions.

Three Ways to Lasting Happiness for Kids

We all love fleeting happiness. It feels fantastic in the moment. The challenge we face with it is that the moment leaves quickly, and unhappiness shows up at the door. The following are ways to strengthen your children's growing sense of lasting happiness so they don't have to go from joy, to pain, to joy, to pain.

#1— *Caring for Others*

I pray for a more friendly, more caring, and more under-standing family on this planet. To all who dislike suffering, who cherish lasting happiness, this is my heartfelt appeal.

— His Holiness the Fourteenth Dalai Lama

Helping others is a great source of joy and contentment—and is central to nurturing lasting happiness. This is in stark contrast to the self-centeredness that is prevalent in some Western countries—caring only about ones' self without regard to others. For example, how many times have you thought, "What's in it for me?" This type of habitual thinking leads to unhappiness.

Have you ever noticed that the more you place the focus upon helping others, the more there is this "magic" that occurs, and you end up feeling happier. When I have had clients contact me in parental "emergencies" and I was able to help them immediately, I felt a sense of purpose, passion for my work, and enduring contentment. Being a "bridge" to facilitate others' happiness is very rewarding.

Guiding children to help others, share their toys, hold the door open, volunteer as they get older, and participate in a "bigger" way in life are all ways to help them grow a happy heart. Every child can help others in different ways, from playing the piano to creating their own lemonade stand to raising money for a "good cause." It almost doesn't matter what children do to help others, but it's important that they begin somewhere: because it will add goodness to someone's life and happiness to their own.

When you realize that helping others not only feels good, but actually makes you happier, you get motivated. You and your children recognize it's in your "enlightened self-interest" to be of service to others.

Bethany's Breakthrough

You may have heard of Bethany Hamilton, the young woman who was attacked by a shark in Hawaii in 2003 when she was just thirteen. Bethany beat the odds and lived, despite losing her left arm and 60 percent of her body's blood supply. Besides the fact that Bethany went on to surf again and actually won the United National Surfing Championship for surfers under age eighteen, she did something almost equally amazing: She developed a skillful worldview and one that leveraged the power of helping others while she was going through an unhappy time. With some support from others (Building Block Four: Social), Bethany realized that her life wasn't over.

In 2005, Bethany went to Thailand after the tsunami and helped those impacted by that tragedy go into the water again. Since then, she has taken subsequent mission trips to inspire others to "never give up" despite what is happening in their lives (Building Block Five: Spirit).

Bethany had to dig deep within herself and tap her inner strength to not only overcome her injuries but to continue living her life. The Five Building Blocks of Confidence are certainly activated in her life, and instead of diminishing her greatness, her thoughts continue to create experiences that empower her (Building Block Two: Beliefs).

You can see more about Bethany's real-life experience in the movie *Soul Surfer*, or learn more at her website: www.bethanyhamilton.com.

* * *

Everyday Kids

Earlier today, I sat down on the floor with two of my favorite kids: Peyton, my neighbor's eleven year-old daughter, and my friend's son Nicholas. "How do you help others?" I asked them both. "And how does it make you feel?" Nicholas said he donated toys, and he explained how he felt like he'd helped other kids. Peyton said, "I gave about six inches of my hair to Locks of Love." (That's an organization that creates hairpieces for children in the United States who have lost hair due to an illness.) "I felt great," she continued, "like I was really helping!"

Both kids felt good after helping others. They realized that by helping others, you truly feel better and happier, too. Guiding kids like Peyton and Nicholas toward the direct experience of helping someone and recognizing how good it feels is step one in planting the seeds of other-centeredness.

#2—Using Challenges as Opportunities

Even a happy life cannot be without a measure of darkness, and the word "happy" would lose its meaning if it were not balanced by sadness. It is far better to take things as they come along with patience and equanimity.

—Carl Jung

One sunny, winter day years ago, I was watching Madeline, my neighbor's child who was four years old at the time. She was a bundle of energy and wanted to use everything as a trampoline. She ran into the living room, fell head first into the square coffee table, and got a large gash in her forehead. I rushed her to the emergency room. Thank goodness all she needed was a few stitches!

As you can imagine, I was scared and uncertain when Madeline was injured. But with time and understanding, I began to learn how to "see" the truth of every situation—that every circumstance, especially the ones I couldn't possibly understand, forced me to grow. We all need to figure out a way to use life's obstacles as fodder for a happy life.

I also came to realize there is nothing against me. Not the economy, increasing gas prices, unexpected trips to the hospital, or loss of a loved one. Through studying and years of experience, I have come to understand that each event of our lives leads us to growth—some softly and others with more force—so that we can truly be the person we came here to be. The goal is learning how to see events in our lives as neutral—or, even better yet, as forces to move us to expand our minds and hearts. Pema Chodron, an American-born Buddhist nun, captured this concept:

> Everything is material for the seed of happiness, if you look into it with inquisitiveness and curiosity. The future is completely open, and we are writing it moment to moment. There always is the potential to create an environment of blame—or one that is conducive to loving-kindness.

To children, negative events—whether a divorce or a broken elbow—don't feel neutral. They feel awful. But you can guide children to see situations as opportunities to expand their hearts to themselves and others. If your child has a broken arm and can't go swimming, for example, he or she can find alternative ways to self-nurture: reading a new series of mystery books, watching science documentaries about outer space, or going for a nature walk.

We all have to learn how to use challenges as stepping-stones to inner confidence; the sooner we do, the more likely we are to find lasting happiness.

Billy's Bully

Bullies have always existed, both on the playgrounds and in board-rooms. Seeing someone being bullied is commonplace for kids. As in generations before, the traditional bullies steal lunch money, lock someone in a locker, put a classmate's head in the sink, or use physical force.

Eight-year-old Billy became my client last school year because he was being bullied by his classmate Jared. Jared pulled down Billy's pants in the lunchroom in front of everyone; he dunked Billy's head in the toilet during playtime and flushed the commode; and he spit spitballs at Billy during class. The torment mortified Billy and certainly shook his sense of confidence.

Our first goal was for Jared to leave Billy alone, but we also worked on how Billy could develop inner strength and set clear no-nonsense boundaries and use this experience as fodder for a happy life. For Billy, learning how to stand up to Jared and strengthen himself from the inside out seemed life-changing.

Our work together wasn't necessarily easy. From comments his teacher made, Billy believed that he wasn't "good enough." So we began our work together debunking his misperceptions of unwor-thiness and his low self-esteem, and then I taught Billy new ways to think about this situation (Block Two: Beliefs) and how these new thoughts would bring inner strength (Block Three: Feelings).

Transforming his thoughts and developing the ability to create positive healthy boundaries—telling this bully to scram when he even came close to Billy—helped Billy, but his success really happened when he created positive confidence feedback loops and turned the energy from feeling terrible (bully experience) into energy he used to create a happier day (Block Four: Social).

Daily affirmations along with our weekly sessions affirmed in

Billy his inner strength and capabilities. He said to me recently, "Moe, thanks! You have really helped me. I know I am a cool dude and can stand up for myself now." This is a big change from the boy I met months earlier who was shaken by this unwanted bully. (Jared the bully is long gone, by the way.)

#3—Calming the Mind

To achieve that state of lasting happiness
and absolute peace, we must first know how to
calm the mind, to concentrate and go beyond the mind.

—Swami Sivananda, Hindu teacher and Yogi

A third way to lasting happiness is learning how to respond to life calmly. Instead of being quickly swayed by negative emotions like anger, your child can connect with his or her calm center and make smart choices when life requires it—like when a beloved pet dies or a sibling breaks a favorite toy.

The best way to teach children about calmness is through your example. Erin, a mother of three, worked closely with me to learn how to respond to life in a calmer way. She "knew" that yelling at her kids wasn't the best response, but she didn't have other emotional tools in her toolbox when situations arose. I shared some techniques with her that worked for me, like breathing exercises, affirmations, and prayer.

For instance, I taught Erin the "Hot Soup Breath," a breathing technique to help release stress and frustration. You take air gently in your nose, hold, and blow out your mouth as if you are cooling hot soup. (Usually, this is done for a minimum of three deep breaths.) When Erin started to get really hot under the collar—when toys littered the living room, her toddler wouldn't listen, her preschool-aged son, Aidan, would ignore her—she stopped what she was doing, breathed nine Hot Soup Breaths, and then felt her calmness.

One day when Aidan was angry, he didn't throw his typical temper tantrum. Instead, he stopped, said "I can do some Hot Soup Breaths like Mommy," and then breathed, while his mom watched with great satisfaction.

As we lead calmer, drama-free lives, our children can do the same. They can respond to experiences in a healthier way.

Changing your habitual tendencies to yell, scream, spank, or respond to life in a less than optimal way takes an inwardly strong parent. The good news is that inner strength is there for you—it is solely a matter of physically (Block One), mentally (Block Two), and emotionally (Block Three) coming into alignment with the power of your being. You can make skillful choices, and by doing so, you can lead your child in that same direction.

For happiness to last, it needs to come from a calm place—a place that knows even among the challenges of everyday living (pain, change, disappointment, rejection), inside of each of us there is that essence that is perfect, complete, and divine.

Susan's "Peace Corner"

I've visited countless schools over the years, from little preschools in small Arkansas towns to the posh private schools with their own animal petting farms in the Hamptons. I've seen a lot of approaches to educating children on what is deemed important, from the three Rs (reading, writing, and arithmetic) to Yoga for first graders.

Susan is a preschool director I met in Englewood, New Jersey, who directs a leading-edge program for preschoolers. Along with making these youngsters "school ready," she teaches character development, social etiquette, emotional health, and confidence.

One of the key aspects of her emotional health program is a Peace Corner that she's implemented in every classroom—a place where boys and girls go to "calm down" when they're upset about something. In this corner, they listen to calming music through a headset, read picture books, play with plush toys, or calm down using breathing exercises.

Jackson, one of the "wild kids" in their classroom, was running around and accidently knocked Jenna on the floor when I was visiting. Jenna scraped her knee and started to cry. Jackson felt terrible; after apologizing to Jenna, he went to the Peace Corner and listened to calming music with his eyes closed. He is learning that he has the capability to calm his mind and feel more peaceful, regardless of what is going on in the outer world.

With regular practice, every healthy child has the power to directly experience that peaceful place within him or her. It is that place that transcends time and space. Directly experiencing that place within helps children better understand their power, and with training, more and more children (and parents, too) can learn how to respond from this calm (and happier) place.

Stillness Speaks

One of the age-old methods of calming the mind is meditation. Parents and teachers frequently ask me, "What is the best meditation?" My response never changes: "The meditation that works for you."

I vividly remember leading a walking meditation for parents and kids in Connecticut, where I guided everyone to put their attention into their mindful movements, walk slowly, quietly notice the birds, fill up the birdfeeders gently, hang prayer flags with awareness, and pick raspberries for an afternoon dessert to celebrate our Sunday.

After the walking meditation, the kids said they felt calmer because:

- Nature is relaxing
- Walking allows "jumpiness" to go away
- Feeding the birds and picking up sticks felt good
- Mimicking someone is easy (following the meditation leader)

Walking quietly and mindfully in a group creates a strong stream of positive energy. (This kind of meditation won't work for every child, but hyperactive kids need something other than sitting on a mat to calm their minds.) One of the young boys spoke with me after the walk: "Moe, thanks!" he said. "I think I felt the Buddha out there. It was great, and now I can do that anytime." I was delighted because I knew this new skill of walking meditation and the habit of going to that peaceful place inside will only help him become stronger from the inside out.

Happier Every Day

> *Being happy is something you have to learn.*
> *I often surprise myself by saying, "Wow, this is it.*
> *I guess I'm happy. I got a home I love. A career I love.*
> *I'm even feeling more and more at peace with myself."*
>
> —Harrison Ford

Inner confidence and lasting happiness aren't biological gifts from great parents; they are developed through practice. They're both skills to master—as learnable as Harrison Ford suggested above. It is our work on Planet Earth to be the person we came here to be, and that can only happen by developing our sense of inner confidence.

Confidence is therefore step one. The work of every effective parent is to help their children believe in themselves—because when children believes in themselves, they expresses the unique gifts that they came to give. This boost in self-confidence also can be used to move forward on the path to creating this deeper form of happiness, too.

Lasting happiness and inner confidence are also dynamic creations, not an all-or-nothing proposition. It isn't a question of having them 100 percent or not at all, because they come in stages; you get a "taste" of that sense of enduring happiness inside, and you practice at making that mindset grow.

Some popular ways to spark this mindset along with growing confidence include:

- Finding a happiness teacher
- Learning (and avoiding) the causes of unhappiness
- Meditating
- Helping others
- Cultivating compassion
- Feeling peace physically (through something like kid's yoga)
- Encouraging your child's interests

Understanding the things that cause your child to create a deeper type of happiness and guiding him or her to do and understand them is nurturing lasting happiness. This means you are mindfully raising your child to "go toward" inner peace and claim his or her power. Author Nathaniel Hawthorne wrote, "Happiness is like a butterfly which, when pursued, is always beyond our grasp, but if you will sit down quietly, may alight upon you."

Creating lasting happiness happens faster when you're not running after it. You simply connect with the people and wisdom that can lead you and your children there—and do the everyday things that increase this deeper sense of peace. Before you know it, you'll get a taste and really appreciate the fact that it was there for you all along.

It's also worth noting that lasting happiness is a sophisticated subject; some thinkers have spent an entire lifetime studying it. The aim of this chapter is solely to introduce the subject and reveal to you how lasting happiness is dependent upon the first step: the creation of inner confidence.

Growing Happy Kids: The Key Messages

Understanding the connection between inner confidence and lasting happiness is often an *aha!* moment for many adults. You now realize that to sow the seeds of your child's deepest type of happiness, you must encourage the cultivation of inner confidence. Here are the main points to remember:

- **Inner confidence** precedes lasting happiness. If you want your child to develop the deepest type of happiness, they need to become strong from the inside out (also known as developing inner confidence).

- **Fleeting happiness** is common in Western children. It is the type of happiness that comes and goes: a child is happy when she has ice cream, but when over the ice cream is gone, her happiness evaporates.

- **Lasting happiness** happens from calming the mind, connecting to wisdom, and cultivating a positive mindset that puts the causes of lasting happiness in place. Cultivating the discipline to calm the mind, connect to wisdom, and establish a skillful (positive) mindset takes an inwardly strong person.

A truly happy person comes through the same dirt of life that everyone else does; he or she has just figured out how to turn toward the metaphorical sun of wisdom and optimism.

Every healthy parent and child has the capability to develop this deeper type of happiness. The time has come to debunk the illusion that genuine happiness is for only some people living on a mountaintop in some foreign land. Lasting happiness can happen for anyone who has the intention, determination, and passion to live the life of their dreams—and help their kids do the same!

part three

Inner Confidence for Every Kid

6

Outer Confidence: Stepping-Stone to Success

I was always looking outside of myself for strength and confidence, but it comes from within. It was there all along.

—Anna Freud

One spring afternoon, my phone rang. When I picked it up, I heard the voice of a hesitant mother on the other end. "Is this Maureen Healy?" she asked. She went on to describe her situation: "My eight-year-old daughter, Dalia, just got 'voted off' the lunchroom table. Her friends were mimicking a reality television show, and now Dalia is a mess—what do I do?"

These third-graders were imitating the then-popular television show *Survivor*, which voted a contestant off the island every week. Dalia's classmates were playing Uno when they decided to vote the poorest player off the table—that was when Dalia got the boot. Since she'd trusted her friends and felt at ease with them, Dalia's growing sense of confidence was shattered when they voted her off the table.

As I spoke with Dalia's mother, I was reminded that parents don't just need to know how to create confidence in their children, but also how to restore confidence once it's been broken. That's what we'll cover in this chapter. I'll share the "warning signs" of wobbly confidence, discuss the common causes of broken confidence in children, and describe how to course-correct toward inner confidence.

In Dalia's situation, she did regain her sense of confidence with her mother's assistance. She was able to see the "truth" of this situation and eventually forgive the "mean girls" who caused her so much heartache. Her sense of confidence also became rooted differently— she learned to stop looking only to other people for validation (outer confidence) and began a practice of looking within herself as a source of power (inner confidence).

Next, we'll explore together how confidence breaks in children and what you can do to help them. These little ones don't need to stay or "get stuck" in outer confidence; preferably, you'll guide them on how to use any experience (good, bad, or indifferent) as a stepping stone to their personal success, deepest strength, and happiest day.

How Confidence Breaks

Confidence breaks when someone (like a parent, teacher, or peer) or something (such as school grades or team tryouts) that your child trusts sends him or her a message that suggests he or she isn't capable or able to do something. This is where the seed of self-doubt is planted. Once children feel doubtful about their capabilities and don't receive any feedback to the contrary (for example, coaching from parents or other adults), their subconscious minds, always on the lookout for answers, begin to suspect that message may be true.

If the outer world then suggests they aren't capable through teasing siblings, poor grades, or being left out, negative self-talk usually
starts. This kind of thinking sounds like:

"I stink at _____ (math, softball, cartwheels)."
"I am not good enough."
"There must be something wrong with me."
"I don't fit in."
"I can't do it."

Young children are highly sensitive to what others say to them. To
a child who loves to draw, an offhanded comment like "You really are
not Picasso" has the power to crush a child's confidence in his artistic
ability and aspirations. Budding artist Billy believes his father (why
wouldn't he? That's his father) and decides his creative abilities are
bunk. Drawing used to be a source of play and fun, but now he's shy
about creating his images.

Offhanded comments and things said without much awareness
still place a weight on a child's heart. They may sound harmless,
but often they are not. The best thing we can do is to become more
mindful so that our thoughts, speech, and actions send positive messages for instilling confidence in our children.

Trusting the important people in their lives is necessary so kids
can form healthy attachments and relationships and feel comfortable
to expand mentally, emotionally, and physically. But when a child
begins school, it is necessary to emphasize self-trust first, and then
guide her to trust others (parents, teachers, and coaches)—those
who will empower her instead of those who will tear down her growing sense of confidence.

Outer Confidence

I cannot always control what goes on outside.
But I can always control what goes on inside.

—Wayne Dyer

Confidence that is broken easily is outer confidence. Since everything in the outer world changes, you cannot consistently develop a
faith in yourself by looking outside of yourself. It just doesn't work.
Imagine you are a movie star, and your sense of confidence is completely dependent upon how much your last movie grosses. But
movie revenues go up and down; outer confidence like this stinks
because it just sets you up for disappointment.

There is typically a defining moment like Billy's that changes a
child's course of self-confidence; in his case, Billy believed that
everything his father said was true. You may remember mine from
earlier in this book: the moment my mother asked me, "Why aren't
you more like the neighbor's daughter?" and I immediately lost a
belief in myself.

Children's confidence is very fragile in the beginning. A child
looks to others to see his or her capabilities, talents, and future abilities in this world. And if growing children have many "moments"
that keep telling them that they aren't highly capable, talented, and
skilled right now, they begin to feel insecure in their world. Even
worse, they start forming low confidence feedback loops.

A child who doesn't start off feeling strong internally will inces-
santly look to others to gain a sense of self-confidence, either through
school grades, sporting wins, or other outer accomplishments. It is
the best they can do with what they've got.

But as I mentioned, nothing stays the same in the outside world.

A child's grades will go up and then fall. Sporting teams win tournaments and then somehow hit a losing streak. A teenager's face breaks out with acne, and then it clears. Nothing in the outer world is permanent or unchanging.

It is for this reason that outer confidence alone always leads to disappointment. Because invariably things on the outside fall apart, and kids who look *exclusively* to the outside world will also fall apart if they rely completely on "outer" things like grades, nice clothes, and accomplishments in the world to show them their magnificence.

The Winner Twins

Brianna and Brittany are identical twin sisters whom I met while writing this book. I found their story so compelling that I want to share it with you here.

In 1995, the girls were born eleven weeks prematurely and survived the challenge of entering the world with low birth weights of about 3 pounds, 9 ounces each and fragile systems. But these wouldn't be the only challenges the girls faced. By fourth grade, these girls not only knew they had dyslexia but defined themselves by it.

Such a misperception is common in childhood. Both Brianna and Brittany are creative and had earlier successes singing at the Junior Olympics and starting a stationery company respectively, but by fourth grade, they had begun to give their power away and looked to the outside world for validation of their capabilities. The challenge came when both girls got failing grades and began to believe they were stupid. This is outer confidence at its worst, because it kept the girls from being able to acknowledge the truth of their powerful beings.

The good news is their father couldn't stand the situation. He realized his girls were smart, capable, and powerful right now. He just needed a way to help the girls realize their abilities, and he recognized that both Brianna and Brittany were excellent storytellers. He told his daughters, "We are writing a book together, and that's it." That was in 2004, when the girls were in fourth grade.

After that, Brianna and Brittany came home from school every day, worked with a tutor, and completed their homework. Then the fun began. The girls cocreated a story, their father transcribed it, and their first book was published in 2008. It was through this direct experience of completing *The Strand Prophecy* with their father, earning royalties, and then winning book awards (including The Benjamin Franklin Book Award for best adolescent fiction) that their self-confidence was bolstered.

These girls no longer look to the outside world for validation of their intelligence, power, and capabilities—they have learned to look within. So much so that with their royalty earnings, the girls have created a nonprofit organization called Motivate2Learn (www.motivate2learn.org), and now they travel around the United States speaking to over 30,000 students each year about how everyone is smart and can overcome any obstacles.

Brianna explained, "I really hope that we are able to inspire kids, especially because of our journey." I believe it is their honesty and their willingness to share their insights and truth that has the power to inspire other children to overcome challenges and develop greater levels of self-confidence.

Signs of Shaky Confidence

Brianna and Brittany both rooted their confidence in their grades. And once they began consistently failing at school, they told their parents, "The other kids are smarter than we are." It was this statement that was a clear sign that their confidence was on shaky ground.

Shaky self-confidence manifests in a few different ways. If you see these signs, I suggest paying careful attention to your child. You may find out that he or she is merely going through a tentative phase of development such as wearing her first bra or getting new braces. Your child may be extra shy because of this new and awkward situation, but with support he or she will emerge with self-confidence.

Of course, the more signs of shaky confidence you see, the more likely there's "something there" that needs to be redirected toward inner confidence. These are some common signs to watch for:

- **Reluctance to Try New Things or Meet New People.** Children who are occasionally hesitant aren't a cause for concern, but children who are consistently reluctant to try new things and risk failing, remaining in their "comfort zone" instead, may not feeling very confident about their abilities. Celebrating each time children try something new (even if they don't like it or they fail) is important—it encourages them to keep trying new things and understand that they are safe in the world.

  Being comfortable meeting new people is also a sign of high confidence. The child who doesn't want to meet new people may have a shy personality or may be experiencing self-doubt or uncertainty. If your son or daughter never wants to meet new people, it's a problem—dealing with new faces is a necessity for connecting and forming healthy relationships. Interacting with strangers doesn't have to be your kid's forte, but it's an important skill to master.

- **Spending Most of His or Her Time Alone.** Christopher loves painting by himself. He participates in painting classes and joins in when necessary, but he prefers to spend time alone. This is a sign of high confidence. Many highly sensitive children prefer to be by themselves or avoid crowds; there's nothing wrong with that preference.

But the child who spends almost all of his or her time alone because he or she is sad, feels unworthy, unlovable, or unskilled is experiencing both low self-esteem and low confidence. Of course, you can have self-esteem or confidence without having both, but they seem to go hand in hand with children who seclude themselves. Sometimes this happens because of a "challenging" family dynamic, like a terminally ill parent, a lack of encouragement from parents to connect with other kids through activities like sports, scouts, or music lessons, or a distorted self-image as unlovable, unworthy, and unskilled. The point is that every healthfully developing child must learn how to positively spend time alone and be with others regardless of their personal preference.

- **Difficulty with Friendships.** Lucy, one of my child clients who is eight years old, has difficulty keeping friendships. She often feels insecure about who she is and what her capabilities are. Unlike most kids who just want to play, Lucy has a rather "heavy" energy, and it is difficult for her to lighten up.

  After we worked together for several months, Lucy let go of many of her limiting beliefs about herself and started seeing herself as strong. I worked with Lucy along with her foster parents so everyone could be on the same "emotional page" and nurture Lucy's growing confidence in ways that work for her. Specifically, we got Lucy into an afterschool activity that she loved (ceramics) and it enabled her to make friends more easily and also "see" herself mastering something that immediately added to her sense of self-confidence.

- **Speaking Poorly About Self.** Charlie, a client of mine, is struggling through his fifth-grade science class and got a 68 on his latest exam. He said to his mother, "Mom, I hate science, and I am so bad at it. I am stupid." This clearly was a red flag indicating that Charlie was catastrophizing his poor grade in science class and extending that lack of confidence to the core of his being. He didn't realize that everyone has certain interests and talents unique to them; we are not necessarily supposed to be good at everything.

This is a perfect example of a child rooting his confidence in the outer world. Charlie let his grades define him and dictate whether or not he was a smart child. Children like this can greatly benefit from learning how to go within and connect with stories of how powerful they are and the potential they have inside of them—just because they are human. It is only then that this looking outside can end, and the true journey inward can begin.

- **Low Expectations.** Daniel, another one of my clients, doesn't have faith in his abilities to accomplish physical tasks, like making it all the way up a climbing wall, lifting some minor weights, or completing a local ropes course. At age eleven, he already expects things not to work out for him. This is a warning sign of wobbly confidence.

   Experience tells me that we get what we expect. For example, I expected the book in your hands to reach parents and now it is doing just that. I didn't expect it from a place of ego and grandiosity, but from a place that knows my unique talent in the world is in nurturing children, helping parents, and communicating messages to them through writing, speaking, and counseling.

   Think about your own life. What happened recently that occurred exactly as you expected? The same is true for a child's life. Guiding children to expect great things for themselves is serious business. The more a child expects herself to succeed at something, the more the chances of that happening skyrocket.

- **Physical Signs.** Slouching and not standing tall are signs of insecurity in the body. It doesn't mean that your son or daughter is automatically lacking in confidence if he or she has poor posture, but if a physically strong child repeatedly has been taught to stand taller or walk with more strength, and he continues to hobble along, his body is sending a very real message. His confidence is shaky and is rooted in outer things that aren't mirroring his magnificence back to him.

Years ago, I had a first-grade student named Uniquea who walked into the room with such confidence that everyone noticed. She looked self-assured; she stood up straight, and her clothes were always nicely pressed, never stained or slovenly. These outer things add to a child's growing sense of confidence and nudge them to begin believing they are powerful.

Signs of wavering confidence aren't confined to this list. These are just the most common indicators that a child is experiencing a shaky sense of confidence. I have found children often saying, "I am stupid" or "I can't do it" when they begin to waver on their abilities. My experience has also demonstrated to me that children who are consistently hesitant to try new things—whether playing a board game, painting a picture, or doing a cartwheel on the front lawn—tend to be acting out of fear instead of faith. Inner confidence is when you have unremitting faith in yourself and your abilities.

Shaky Situations

Children experience life anew all the time. Experiences that may seem average and regular to us are completely amazing to them. That is part of the joy of being with children. You get to see the world through their eyes and remember how everything really is a miracle, from seeing hummingbirds to hearing a helicopter overhead. It all feels truly awesome.

But there are also moments in childhood that challenge a child's sense of self. These are what I call shaky situations, when children feel unsure of themselves and their capabilities. I can still remember my first day of Girl Scouts, which just happened to be the start of their cookie drive! *Oh my goodness*, I thought. *Can I do this? How do I sell cookies? Will my parents help?*

Moments that shake a child's self-confidence are common. You can probably anticipate them, too. Some of the universal ones include:

- Starting a new school
- Making new friends
- Failing a test
- Being teased (or bullied)
- Peer rejection
- Not making a sports team
- Change in physical appearance (including braces, new haircut, pimples, or a broken arm)
- Parental criticism
- Being different (for example, having a learning disability)
- Mastering a new skill (like selling cookies)

These are the everyday moments that might require extra care and feeding to nurture your child's development of inner confidence. You'll likely notice that all of these shaky situations have one thing in common: they are grounded in Outer Confidence. Your children are seeking to find validation of their capabilities from the outer world, from getting straight A's to selling the most candles in the school fundraiser. Your role is to guide them back to the truth of their powerful being inside of them.

Course-Correcting

You may notice your son or daughter is showing signs of "wobbly confidence." What should you do? Like an airline pilot, keep course correcting toward your destination. Of course, the destination is inner confidence, but in realistic terms, you want to see your child show signs of inner confidence.

Course-correcting a child's low sense of self-confidence includes:

• Plugging your child back into the Five Building Blocks of Confidence
• Identifying the Block that isn't working for your child
• Guiding your child to let go of what's not working, and replace it with a thought that seeds inner confidence

This can be a tricky endeavor, especially with children who have repeatedly used negative self-talk and believe that they aren't highly capable today.

Geoff, a ten-year-old client of mine, got into the habit of saying, "I can't do it" whenever there was something new to try. His mother, Betty, brought him to me precisely for this reason. She explained, "I can't get through to Geoff that he can do whatever he puts his mind to, and for some reason he stays stuck in believing that he can't do it." So this was our starting point.

Why was Geoff stuck? After many sessions together, it turned out that Geoff's father, who he idolized, had dismissed Geoff's desire to be a musician. His dad said, "You'll never make it as a drummer so you better stay in school." Instead of not believing his father, Geoff assumed that he was right—and unfortunately extended his disbelief into other things he was trying.

Unwinding this primary programming is essential to get Geoff back on the confidence track so that he can move forward with a better sense of himself and his capabilities. In this instance, I identified that it was his false beliefs (Block Two) that diminished his sense of self-confidence. Once the root of "wobbly" confidence is found, the rest is about figuring out how to remove that weed. Geoff and I worked together for months; I shared my experiences and gave him lessons about confidence as well as some homework, including visualizations, affirmations, and listening to his favorite music.

One day he had a breakthrough. He'd decided to try out for the basketball team, and on the morning of tryouts, Betty walked into his room and found Geoff sitting at his desk, saying "I can do it" aloud and visualizing himself making the team.

Geoff's path to inner confidence is just beginning. One of the larger parts of ensuring that it happens on a step-by-step basis was involving Betty in the Five Building Blocks of Confidence. It is through this system that Betty began to understand how Geoff's confidence got sidetracked and how she can nurture it more regularly.

In the next chapter, I share my "Three-Step Process" for turning a negative thought to a positive thought.

Broken Blocks

A break in any one of the Blocks can impede a child's development of confidence and limit his or her ability to become inwardly confident. As a review, the Blocks are:

- **Block One**—Biology is the foundational Block. If a child is persistently plagued by depression, mood disorders, or other severe emotional challenges then confidence isn't possible until this is rectified. Some of the other ways a child's biology also gets compromised is through poor nutrition, lack of sleep, and not enough regular exercise.

• **Block Two**—Beliefs are the creator Block. What children think is going
to dictate their sense of self-confidence that emerges from the core of
their being. The sooner children root their confidence internally versus
externally, the faster they will "fall back" on the idea that within them is
the power to succeed no matter what. For example, Jenny was trying out
for the third-grade basketball team, and she missed the shot. Instead
of saying "I can't do it," she said, "Let me try again! I know I can do it,"
because she has a growing sense of inner confidence.

If you hear your child saying "I can't do it," then this Block (Beliefs)
needs to be course-corrected toward inner confidence.

• **Block Three**—Emotions are the amplifier Block. It is this Block where
a child thinks a certain thought and feels the emotion corresponding to
it. For example, a child can think "Boy, I stink at football" and this surely
has a down-in-the-dumps emotional correlate. Conversely, thinking
"WOW, I rock at swimming" and feeling that course through your
veins creates an incredibly positive and empowered feeling. Emotions
are what strengthen a child's sense of confidence or doubt.

If you see your child looking disappointed, sad, and rejected about
his or her poor performance, then you know Block Two (Beliefs) and
Block Three (Emotions) are showing his or her lack of inner confidence.
Time again to course-correct.

• **Block Four**—Social is the reinforcement Block. Children begin to
engage themselves in positive or negative self-talk (intrapersonal)
or hear from others (interpersonal) how they are capable, talented,
and have great potential—or the opposite. These repeated forms of
inner or outer feedback are considered confidence feedback loops that
strengthen a child's emerging sense of confidence or doubt. Consider
for a moment the child who repeatedly hears "Great job on making
your bed!" versus the one who hears "You aren't doing it right." It's

no surprise the child who hears positive feedback about his or her capabilities has an easier time of building self-confidence.

If your child tells you repeatedly about the teacher who says, "You aren't very good in Spanish," then you can step in to course-correct this negative outer feedback. This will also help shift a child's inner feedback to something more positive as he or she gets confidence-building feedback from outside.

• **Block Five**—Spiritual is the expander Block. (This is the only Block not *required* for confidence.) Children who believe in "something greater" and also believe that greatness is within them have an easier time activating inner confidence. The focus is on leading children to see and believe in their inherent divinity and power within. If your son or daughter develops a sense of "blind faith" in a God up on a mountaintop, this is not helpful for strengthening inner confidence—children must believe that power of God or the divine is within them.

As we know, children often take things very literally, so if your child tells you that God (or Buddha, Spirit, Divine Love) is in heaven and doesn't reside within him or her (and this is your belief system), you can course-correct him or her to also "know" that the power of God (Spirit, Universe, Divine, Infinite Intelligence, Buddha) is within him or her giving strength in every moment.

Each Block builds upon the previous one, and they are interconnected in their level of functioning. For example, if children believe they are capable of kicking a winning goal into the net (Block Two), but no one encourages or they don't repeatedly talk positively to themselves (Block Four), then this belief is weak, not strong. The creation of inner confidence depends on how strong a child's beliefs are about his or her inner power, strength, and potential.

Bully on the Bus

Second-grader Sarah was feeling sad on the school bus ride home because she'd failed her spelling test. She got off the bus on her regular stop, and an older boy yelled out the bus's window: "Sarah's stupid! Stupido. Stupido. Stupido!"

Sarah didn't turn around as she walked down her block, but she heard every single word, and the tears flowed down her face. She felt even worse now. Did he know she was feeling bad about flunking her spelling test? Did he pick on her because of her sad look? What happened?

When Sarah got home she went straight to her room and cried. She didn't even notice her father welcoming her as she entered the house. Sarah just sat in her room thinking: *I stink. I failed. I am no good. I can't believe David yelled those things at me out the window. Am I stupid?*

Maggie, Sarah's mother, came home from a busy day at the office and yelled a hello to Sarah. When she peered into Sarah's room, Maggie saw her crying. "What's wrong?" she asked. Sarah responded, "Mom, I can't do school anymore. The other kids think I am stupid."

Sarah's confidence was shaken to the core. Maggie called me that evening to see Sarah the next day.

I met with Sarah for four months, and I helped her see her situation differently. She felt like a victim of the circumstances in her life instead of an active participant. To help reframe this situation for Sarah, I:

- Gave her books on overcoming bullies (written by other kids)
- Connected her to other kids who'd overcome bullying
- Assigned her a daily affirmation
- Supported her with weekly sessions (debunking false beliefs and planting new ones)

• Praised her efforts (as she got back on the bus and began studying again)
• Helped her master new things (piano lessons and a pottery class)

Sarah began to see her situation differently after learning more about her bully. She found out her bully just lost his father in an airplane accident, and this helped her feel more compassionate. Sarah also began to understand that mistakes are part of the "success process" and don't reflect anything about her or her abilities. I also partnered with her mother to add more positive confidence feedback loops into her life. Maggie started spending five minutes each morning with Sarah and building up her sense of self-confidence. Sarah loved this!

Because she had relied solely on her grades for confidence, she thought she was a failure when she failed a test. Since we know that outer confidence alone leads to disappointment, it's not surprising that Sarah became very disappointed and even sad. This situation was compounded by the bully calling her "stupido" out the window for everyone to hear.

Sarah's confidence faltered in Block Two: Beliefs. Children's belief about their capabilities and potential direct their sense of self-confidence. Since Sarah began to believe she was a failure and was questioning her skills and doubting her abilities, it's logical that her confidence plummeted. She no longer felt strong inside, capable and able to succeed at school or life.

Along with not thinking confident thoughts, Sarah felt down in the dumps; here's where Block Three: Emotions broke. Next, ruminating about how she failed and why the bully picked on her created a negative confidence feedback loop. Her negative self-talk reinforced the belief of being a failure. Block Four: Social was performing in a negative way—Sarah activated it as a negative confidence feedback loop.

One of the things that Sarah found really helpful was learning how to "stand up" to a bully and not give her power away. I believe it was her direct experience talking to other kids who overcame similar challenges and getting additional support from her mother daily that strengthened her from the inside out. Plus, we focused on what she does well, like playing the piano and making amazing pottery. It didn't take long for Sarah to habitually think more positive thoughts.

The Dance of Doubt

> *If you doubt yourself, then indeed*
> *you stand on shaky ground.*
>
> —Henrik Ibsen

Doubt is the absence of confidence. Instead of thinking and feeling "I can do it!" the opposite is occurring: "I can't do it, and boy do I stink at _____ (fill in the blank)."

Some self-doubt during childhood is natural. Your son or daughter may wonder: *Can I dive into the deep end? Am I ready to take the training wheels off my bicycle? I don't think I can climb that tree.* Since your child hasn't accomplished these things before, this self-doubt is merely highlighting the fact that he or she is on new ground.

You may remember the Emotional Scale of Confidence in Chapter 4, where doubt was sandwiched between fear, insecurity, and uncertainty. It is also diametrically opposite self-love, trust, and inner confidence, thus suggesting foolish self-doubt is what brings confidence down versus bolstering it up.

To help children diminish self-doubt and embrace themselves as more powerful, you can:

1. Acknowledge the situation (Sarah failed her test and was bullied)

2. Debunk doubt (Told Sarah she was powerful and strong inside)

3. Provide new opportunities (Sarah got back on the bus, head held high and the bully left her alone—plus, she started new things like piano lessons)

4. Add positive confidence feedback loops (Sarah's mom praised Sarah's efforts every day, which helped Sarah see herself as powerful)

It's also helpful to be honest with your kids and share that everyone feels fear or uncertainty sometimes. I told Sarah about the first time I rode a mountain bike and stood at the bottom of the mountain looking up. I was scared. But as I was guided by an excellent teacher, I moved forward. Today, I'm an excellent cyclist.

Science Says

If you praise the effort, the strategy a child used,
the perseverance, the improvement—these things
focus on what the child actually did. These are things
the child can do again in the face of difficulty.
You're teaching the child what brought success
in the first place, and what to do again if she stumbles.

—Carol Dweck, Ph.D., author of *Mindset: The New Psychology of Success*

Carol Dweck, a Stanford University professor who has done research with elementary school children in New York City, revealed that if you focus on praising a child's process (efforts, approach, and perseverance), then they tend to have the faith, self-belief, and willingness to stick with challenging situations regardless of outcome.

This is in contrast to praising a child's outcomes (great report card or a clean room) where they learn to solely do those things for which they are praised.

When adults use an inwardly focused praise approach, I have found that children believe in themselves more easily. And since we know that beliefs are the "creators" of inner confidence, this type of praise becomes a powerful accelerator of inner confidence.

For instance, here's some of the "inner praise" I gave Sarah:

- ✓ You really are strong inside for getting back on the bus. I admire your inner strength and determination to make second grade work.
- ✓ By using index cards, you really have learned your spelling words quickly. That was a great approach!
- ✓ Wow, you practiced for forty-five minutes on the piano. It is putting in this type of effort that leads to success.

Shifting how we praise our children from the blanket "great job" to something that acknowledges their inner efforts can contribute mightily to bolstering children's sense of inner confidence. Their confidence is then not based on outer accomplishments, like whether they scored 100 percent on their pop spelling quiz or landed the lead in the school play, because the undercurrent of this praise is "You Can Do It."

As you praise children's efforts and process, they come to believe that inside of them is something that can succeed. It doesn't depend upon outcome, and it is something they can tap into whenever they need it. When faced with obstacles and challenges, they begin remembering that they can do it.

By praising a child repeatedly, you are forming a positive confidence feedback loop. It is this type of loop that strengthens a child's growing sense of confidence. Of course, this is especially important if a child's confidence breaks, and you are in the process of "course-correcting" so he or she heads back in the direction to inner confidence.

Cultivating Outer and Inner Confidence— So Happy Together!

Believe in yourself and all that you are. Know there is something inside of you greater than any obstacle.

—Christian D. Larson, New Thought teacher and leader

When Brianna and Brittany Winner relied solely on their grades for confidence, they came up short. The same thing also happened with Sarah when she failed her spelling test. You and I have probably learned this same experience time and time again. The good news is that since we are raising children today in a completely new way, they don't have to experience the pain of relying on only outer confidence. Our kids get to be raised in the awareness that everything they accomplish in the "outside world" is merely a representation of their inner power, strength, and potential.

Cultivating outer confidence while planting the seeds of inner confidence is the most skillful path to power. So as your child masters something in the outer world, like getting good grades, playing the piano, writing a story, setting the table, making a card, or saying his or her alphabet correctly for the first time, celebrate this outer success while also pointing them inward. You can say, "John, great job at memorizing the alphabet! You are powerful and can use that power to do anything in this world."

One of my clients, Aidan, just started at a new school in fourth grade. He was feeling very nervous about this experience. I coached him on how to introduce himself to kids and make new friends. Of course, I reminded him that all of these outer things feel good, but what's most important is that he believe in himself. He said, "Moe, I take deep breaths at the bus stop and say to myself, 'I have superhero strength.'" I complimented Aidan on this because it builds his growing sense of outer and inner confidence simultaneously.

The Path to Inner Confidence

Faith in oneself . . . is the best and safest course.

—Michelangelo

Outer confidence is a necessary step toward inner confidence. But if your children stop at outer confidence, relying on only outer things like grades, friends, clothes, and the latest gadgets to show them their magnificence, they'll always be disappointed because things change, break, or go away. After all, the nature of life is ever-changing, and guiding your child to have a stable inner sense of confidence is the safest course to developing his or her resilience, strength, and power. With a deeper belief in themselves, children can learn how to overcome obstacles and use their energy to succeed in life.

My path toward inner confidence and personal power moved me to discover Eastern wisdom and contemporary spirituality, and claim that the divine spark that created the world is that same energy within me.

In the next chapter, I share with you how to create this deeper form of inner confidence, especially after your child's confidence has been shaken. You, as your child's primary example, will learn empowering ways for yourself—and you will be guided to nurture this deeper form of confidence in your child.

We'll also reconnect to the Five Building Blocks of Confidence in a new way and peel back another layer on what the thoughts are that create inner confidence. Because if you can think the thoughts of inner confidence, you can feel the feelings—and when you get to feeling the feelings, it's just a matter of plugging back into the proven system.

So onward and upward we go!

7

Inner Confidence: Planting Stronger Seeds

It is faith that steers us through stormy seas;
faith that moves mountains, and faith that jumps
across the ocean. That faith is nothing but a living
and wide-awake consciousness of God within.

—Gandhi

What I am guiding you to share with your children is that they can have faith in themselves—they can begin to develop a belief that within them there is a power to succeed no matter what. I found the easiest way to lead children to more fully embrace their potential, power, and capabilities today is to teach them about the Source, God, Power, or Buddha Seed within. Regardless of the name you use to describe their inner strength, the important point is that you lead your children beyond their perceived mistakes, disappointments of everyday life, and constant seeking for approval in outer things like grades to something deeper. This something deeper is where they learn to develop an avid faith and reliance on themselves.

In the previous chapter, we learned how to see the signs of wobbly self-confidence and what we can do to course-correct them. Every child naturally feels a little uncertain when things come up that are completely new, like starting at a new school or learning how to ride a bike without training wheels. (Remember the first time you took the training wheels off your bike? I can, and it was terrifying.)

But with practice, we learn how to think more inwardly confident thoughts and let go of negative thoughts that keep us playing small. In this chapter, I share a three-step process that has helped countless children move from that habitual place of feeling "I can't do it" to something more expansive and empowering like, "Oh, yes I can!" Throughout the course of raising a more confident child, you'll probably need to transform one of his or her thoughts from something shaky to something stronger, and this Three-Step Process can help with that.

Along with this Three-Step Process, I also profile three types of children who often need extra assistance in cultivating inner confidence. They are The Wounded Child, The Highly Sensitive Child, and The Exceptional Child—and they can sprout strength like any other child (just with a little more help).

So come with me on this journey of nurturing self-confidence at an even deeper level, strengthening it, and supporting our children in thinking thoughts that empower them—especially after they've had a few bumps.

Struggle to Strength

Where there is no struggle, there is no strength.

—Oprah Winfrey

Using a struggle as an opportunity to create a sense of inner strength is commendable . . . however, you needn't struggle to create strength. I know that you can have strength from thinking inwardly confident thoughts (Block Two), feeling those feelings (Block Three), developing a strong body (Block One), and surrounding yourself with uplifting people who mirror back to you your magnificence (Block Four). I also know that by developing a spiritual practice (Block Five) you get to expand your sense of strength, power, and possibility; this type of experience accesses the infinite and allows the infinite to flow not only to you but through you.

Oprah does make a valid point though. Where there is struggle, there is the opportunity for greater strength. Think of it in energetic terms, such as some "big problem" like your daughter being bullied on the playground.

Jane is upset and feels so deeply hurt. Some older kid named Kai was calling her "Pee Wee" and telling everyone that she wet her pants when she sat on a wet chair by accident. The energy she is using to feel terrible is the same energy she can use to learn how to rechannel to feel great, claim her greatness, and see herself as a powerful child.

So the key to developing inner confidence is not only teaching thoughts of inner confidence, feeling those feelings, surrounding a child with uplifting friends, and pointing a child inward, but guiding your child to realize that she is the creator of her life. Nearly every thought she thinks produces a feeling: If she is feeling down, she can learn to counteract that by thinking differently and therefore producing different feelings. In Jane's situation, when she was on the playground, she was probably thinking: "Everyone is laughing at me. It really looks like I peed myself. I am so embarrassed. This is awful. Why isn't this boy being nice to me?" She was knee-deep in "poor me" thoughts that weren't very empowering.

Jane could have turned things around with new thoughts. She could have thought instead, "I am strong inside. I have superhero strength! I get to choose to feel good now. Kai has problems. He probably feels stinky, too. I'm going to walk away and stay strong. Bye, bye!" This response feels so much better and stronger than the original case scenario.

Children must learn how to create better feeling thoughts. It's instinctual for them to feel hurt when teased, to wonder what is wrong with themselves, and to shrink instead of expand when they aren't treated nicely. Every parent, adult, and teacher can guide children to feel stronger on the inside—whether it is day one of their experience on Planet Earth, or day 1,832 when they are faced with a bully on the playground.

The main lesson is that you show your children through the clarity of your example and through your verbal guidance that any struggle can be used as a stepping stone toward greater strength.

Steps to Strength: The Three-Step Process

As we know, life is a series of challenges for our children—a bully on the playground, a broken toe, or a failed math test—but we can choose how to help them deal with those challenges. What do you do when your child comes home after a hard day? Do you listen? Try to make it better? Talk to him or her to see what the root cause of the situation really is?

These are all good options. But after years of working with children on emotional issues, I have created an effective Three-Step Process that helps you guide your child back to his or her power:

Step One: Identify Misperceptions
The first step of this process is about identification. You must identify where your child's thinking went off the inner confidence path.

Step Two: Remove False Beliefs
Before you can guide your child toward more empowering ideas, you must help remove the false belief (misperception) that was identified in Step One.

Step Three: Add Skillful Beliefs
Add empowering ideas to replace those limiting beliefs that were keeping your son or daughter playing small.

Lily came to me with the regular "scary monster" syndrome at four years of age. Her mother, Cynthia, brought her to me because Lily wasn't sleeping; she thought she was going to be eaten by monsters at night. Lily clearly needed to be thinking more inwardly confident thoughts (as well as learn how to self-soothe).

I used the Three-Step Process with Lily in the following manner:

Step One: Identify Misperceptions

It was clear that Lily believed she wasn't safe at night with the scary monsters in her closet. Instead of "making Lily wrong," I simply listened to her situation and identified what was underlying her fear. I learned that not long ago, she was bitten by a dog. Her fears of not being safe in the world were emerging in the evening. At the same time, her mother was forcing her to stay in her room alone. But the outcome of this first step was that I identified how Lily went off the confidence course: she believed she wasn't safe in the world, and scary monsters were more powerful than she was.

Step Two: Remove False Beliefs

After identifying that Lily felt unsafe in the world and powerless in the face of these monsters, I spoke with Lily about how strong she is from the inside out and that there was nothing in the outer world—not even scary monsters—that could harm her. Of course, I also wanted her to believe me, so I shared my own genuine experience of being convinced of scary things in my own closet when I was just a little older than Lily. I would have my father look in the closet and under the bed and keep the door ajar with the hallway light on every single night. As I got older, I realized that I had great power inside of me, and I understood that the same power that holds the stars in the sky is in me, and also in her. Her eyes opened up wide, and she smiled.

Step Three: Add Skillful Beliefs

My approach with adding skillful beliefs with Lily was from the universal concept that Lily has a power inside of her that can conquer anything. I also gave her breathing exercises to calm herself and music to soothe her worries as well as a crystal to help her feel strong. She said, "Moe, I love this crystal. It reminds me of you. When I feel a little scared, then I remember that I am strong."

Being able to help Lily move past her fears and begin seeing herself as strong again was an important step to helping her regain her confidence. I was also fortunate to assist her mother in refining her parenting approach to support Lily's growing sense of confidence, too. (She helped Lily feel safe again without forcing her to stay in her room and gently guided her to think more empowering thoughts.)

This Three-Step Process can be used by any adult or professional in simply moving a child beyond her fears and helping her begin thinking more inwardly confident thoughts.

Identifying Misperceptions

Here are some common misperceptions that children hold on to that limit their growing sense of inner confidence. I think you'll recognize many of the examples of shaky and outer confidence on the left, and if you hear them from your child, guide him or her to more inwardly confident thoughts such as those provided on the right.

Uncertainty and Outer Confidence	Inner Confidence
I am my grades.	I am greater than my grades. My greatness comes out in every way today.
I am only as good as my last soccer win.	Inside of me is endless power that I can use at any time.
I am stupid.	Within me is the wisdom of the world.
I am not skilled.	My talents are coming out more and more every day.

Uncertainty and Outer Confidence (cont'd)	Inner Confidence (cont'd)
I can't do it.	I can do anything with God's rich help.
I made a mistake.	Every mistake brings me closer to success!
Nobody believes in me.	The whole world is full of people who believe in me, and I believe in me, too!
I am little and small.	Inside of me is great power. I now feel big and strong!

Children hold these common misperceptions because they're seeking their sense of self-worth and confidence externally. When you see these patterns, you can gently guide your child to let go of the limiting thought and replace it with a more inwardly confident belief.

Step by Step

Anthony was shaken up when he came home from preschool. He told his mother, Jeanne, that his friend Mike called him "stinky," and the other kids didn't want to play with him after that. He felt terrible. Anthony said, "Mom, do I smell?" Jeanne leaned in and sniffed the air. "No honey, you're perfect," she replied. But Anthony didn't feel perfect, and he started feeling bad about the whole experience.

When Jeanne called to ask for my help, I suggested that she listen to Anthony's story and focus on the Three-Step Process:

1. Identify Misperceptions
2. Remove False Beliefs
3. Add Skillful Beliefs

Anthony talked to Jeanne while playing with one of his favorite toys—a Tyrannosaurus Rex puzzle. After listening to Anthony this time, Jeanne realized that he—like most kids—wanted his friend and the school to validate that he was a good kid and one who smells just fine. (Jeanne was at Step One by identifying Anthony's false beliefs. His misperception was that it mattered what others thought of him—thus he was giving away his power.)

So Jeanne said, "Honey, you are a perfect child. Did you know that you and the T. Rex are made of God stuff?" Anthony shook his head no. "You see, since you are made of God stuff, you and the T. Rex are powerful beings who are strong inside, and you're amazing creatures regardless of what anyone says!" (This is Step Two where Jeanne is removing the belief that it is important what others think, and also Step Three where she is replacing the false belief with a new, skillful one, adding that the "God stuff" is inside of Anthony.)

As they continued playing, Jeanne explained that the T. Rex did have a distinct smell, just like little kids do. "Smells are good," she told Anthony. "Besides, who cares what other kids say about how we smell anyway?" she added. "We are made of the God stuff, and that makes us perfect in every way!" Anthony smiled; Jeanne could tell he felt stronger inside, and she shared this conversation with me over the phone that night.

The big win came the next day. Anthony's preschool teacher phoned Jeanne at lunch. "What did you do with Anthony last night?" she asked. "He's telling everyone that he and dinosaurs have the God stuff inside, which makes them perfect in every way. Needless to say, all the kids are interested and want to know if they have the God stuff, too!" Jeanne laughed, knowing this was part of the fun of building her son's confidence.

Inner Confidence for Every Child

Inner confidence can happen for any child, even those with bumpy starts, like Wayne Dyer (who grew up in an orphanage) or Louise Hay (a survivor of child abuse). Some children need to heal where they've been before they're able to get to where they're going.

In this section, I'll share three common types of children who might pose challenges for professionals and parents: The Wounded Child (who has experienced trauma, abuse, or loss); The Highly Sensitive Child; and The Exceptional Child.

These children come with some complexities, but also great talents. It is 150 percent worth the effort to help these amazing children discover their unique signature skills of greatness and empower them to bring their gifts to the world.

The Wounded Child

I am not what happened to me,
I am what I choose to become.

—Carl Jung

Staggering numbers of children in the world experience trauma, loss, and abuse on an everyday basis. Bruce Perry, fellow at the ChildTrauma Academy, estimates that just in America, more than 5 million children annually experience a childhood trauma. Of course, a child who has consistently experienced trauma (like sexual or verbal abuse) usually has greater difficulty cultivating any sense of confidence—especially inner confidence.

These traumatized children need to get on the same path to confidence as children with less eventful childhoods. But before they can do so, there are a few preliminary steps that are a necessary foundation for a "wounded child" to get on the course to feeling strong and becoming happier:

- Remove the cause (if possible) of abuse and trauma
- Put the child in a healthier place
- Connect the child to a healer (a therapist or creative arts sessions)

Children who have experienced severe trauma in early development see life differently than children who haven't. Instead of seeing Planet Earth as a safe place full of supportive people, traumatized children often view the world around them as hostile and unfriendly.

Besides exiting the trauma from the child's energetic, mental, and emotional system, a healing professional needs to guide a child into a healthy worldview, in which he or she begins seeing the Universe as a friendly, supportive, and loving place. In order to have faith in yourself, you must believe that the Universe will support you. This is at the heart of healing a wounded child.

A trained professional can help to change these thoughts. Someone who can see what is unseen, like unremitting self-doubt and how it impacts that child, is incredibly important. When a child has complex trauma from early childhood, I've seen success through creative arts therapy or the use of energy medicine to clear away blocks. Creative arts therapy provides an outlet for the wounded child to release stuck energy and unproductive feelings in a healthy way. Then, I believe traditional counseling can be very effective to help a child see how viewing himself or herself as "not good enough" or "not skilled" is really bunk—and the only ones with the problems were the adults who mistreated him or her.

Inner-child work can also be helpful. This is really for older children (or adults) who have experienced deep-seated pain early on. One of my clients, Dawn, tried to kill herself at age seven by taking a tack and attempting to cut her wrist with it. Her family life was full of verbal abuse, and her mother had borderline personality disorder, which meant that one minute she would say "Dawn, I love you," and the next minute say, "Dawn, you were a mistake," sending completely mixed messages.

At twenty-one years old, Dawn was feeling the emotional and energetic effects of her abusive childhood. So I guided her to speak to her "inner child" and ask her what she needed, give her what she never got, and help bring her—when she was ready—to the present time so she could heal her from this emotional wound. This is progressive work for a twenty-one-year-old, but Dawn wanted to feel confident. She did this work to let go of her limiting beliefs through guided meditation and journaling.

Along with creative arts, traditional counselings, and inner child work—Dawn was then ready to plug into the Five Building Blocks of Confidence at a deeper level. She will need consistent use of positive confidence feedback loops like any child from a challenging background but that's a small price to pay for inner power.

The Highly Sensitive Child

> *. . . it is primarily parenting that decides*
> *whether the expression of sensitivity*
> *will be an advantage or source of anxiety.*

—Elaine Aron, psychologist and author of *The Highly Sensitive Child*

Does your child hate the itchy tags inside shirts? Does she like quiet play more than noisy groups? Does he seem to read your mind? Ask lots of questions? Is she incredibly perceptive at noticing all the small details of life? Perhaps he's been called "shy" or "highly emotional" by someone close to him? If so, you may have a highly sensitive child.

Dr. Elaine Aron described highly sensitive children as being "one of the 15–20 percent of children born with a nervous system that is highly aware and quick to react to everything." As a former highly sensitive child, I personally relate to her definition. These children are incredibly responsive to their environments: they are impacted by the lighting, sounds, smells, or overall mood of the people around them.

With a sharpened sense of awareness, these children are often intellectually, creatively, and emotionally gifted; they often demonstrate genuine compassion at early ages. The downside is that these intensely perceptive kids can also become easily overwhelmed by crowds, noises, new situations, sudden changes, and others' emotional distress. My eight-year-old client Lizzie came home from school and broke down crying after witnessing a bullying episode. Criticism, defeat, and the distress of others is something sensitive children feel deeply.

Highly sensitive children often build their confidence more easily when they are raised by sensitive parents, placed in schools that honor their unique gifts, and make friends who are similarly sensitive. If these things happen, these children aren't as likely to hear excessive negative criticism, feel like they don't belong because they're "different" from the other kids, or somehow feel "less than" at school.

Summer, one of my child clients, is a highly sensitive child who attended a traditional public school in Asheville, North Carolina. She felt like a fish out of water, because traditional school systems don't measure a child's level of creativity, sensitivity, and unique gifts. The only classes she enjoyed were art and music; Summer was a gifted violinist who actively contributed to the Asheville music scene. When I met Summer, it became clear that letter grades weren't lifting her confidence. She looked to her grades to reflect back her genius, but they didn't. So I taught her parents about the Five Building Blocks of Confidence, how to nurture inner confidence through empowering songs, and also suggested they move her to a more creative, empowering environment.

Her parents took all of my recommendations, and Summer is now building her sense of confidence from outer to inner with more gusto! She's stopped looking exclusively to the outer world for validation, and she feels supported in a more creative space where she's not considered "weird" but is more like the other children with highly creative, intelligent, and imaginative skills. (An added plus for Summer: there are no letter grades at her new school.)

Highly sensitive children need their surroundings to support their sensitivity and help them see their uniqueness as a gift. They also need the following to build inner confidence:

- Less criticism
- More praise, encouragement, and support
- Surroundings that uplift them
- More understanding from parents, caregivers, teachers, family members, and friends
- Healthy foods
- Inner confidence heroes
- Inspiration

These approaches will help plant inner confidence and allow your unique child to discover his or her strengths with enthusiasm.

The Exceptional Child

Children are likely to live up to what you believe of them.

—Lady Bird Johnson, former First Lady of the United States

Some children come to Planet Earth to learn how to overcome challenges on their path to greatness. Those challenges may come in a physical form, like an illness, lisp, or limp, while other children have different difficulties, like learning challenges such as dyslexia or attention deficit disorder. Whatever your child's path, they can still develop inner confidence.

For many children with these challenges, it's helpful to:

- Focus on their strengths
- Turn those strengths into skills
- Guide them to see their skills

At first, this process will help a child develop outer confidence—a necessary stepping-stone to inner confidence. My six-year-old client Rose has dyslexia, so her parents focused on other things she can do well, like taking care of her parakeet, Peach, and using the video camera to create funny home movies. Rose's parents recognize her ability to care for animals and share an intuitive sense with them, so they take her to visit local wildlife rescue facilities and seek other ways to strengthen her interests. "I'm great with animals and my parents think so, too!" Rose told me. Outer feedback like this strengthens Rose's growing sense of confidence.

The process of creating confidence in children with any type of special challenge is a matter of finding their unique talent and developing it. As they begin to feel more assured about a particular skill (outer confidence) along with having someone in their life guide them to their power (inner confidence), they begin to develop a solid sense of confidence that gets deepened and not destroyed.

This helps children use their "challenge" as a stepping-stone toward their inner strength and confidence. You may remember the Winner twins from the last chapter—they are the perfect examples of children who used their obstacles as a springboard toward a greater level of self-confidence.

Strengthening Kids

Strengthening children to have the courage, strength, and, yes, inner confidence to be the person they came here to be sometimes will take extra effort when children are faced with special challenges.

Highly Sensitive and Exceptional Children are two types of kids who need extra assistance in building their sense of outer and inner confidence. If they've had healthy childhoods without any trauma, these children aren't as complicated as the ones who've witnessed horrific things, been abused, or somehow decided in their development that they were powerless.

Some other types of children you want to keep a keen eye out for and give extra assistance to develop inner confidence include: The Perfectionist, The People Pleaser, and The Depressed Child. These types of children notoriously look to the outer world for a sense of approval and validation of their capabilities.

Of all the "types" of children, I find The Wounded Child often presents the most challenges. This is especially true for those who decided early on that the world isn't safe. They are best served to let go of these negative belief systems through a combination of creative and traditional means. Said differently, a child's subconscious (just below the surface) thoughts will run the show unless they are brought to consciousness and transformed. Confidence is beyond their grasp until this happens.

The Blocks and More

Cultivating this deeper type of strength in your children means you are helping them think the thoughts, feel the feelings, and personally experience their power at even greater levels where they believe that, YES, the power is within them. The fastest way to do this is to leverage the wisdom of the Five Building Blocks of Confidence: Biology, Beliefs, Emotions, Social, and Spiritual.

Along with the Five Building Blocks of Confidence, you can look at the idea of raising children with inner confidence through Eastern wisdom. Specifically, the Buddhist tradition that I am trained in emphasizes ethics, compassion, and wisdom as powerful ways to deepen inner confidence. Let's look at them here:

Ethics

Those individuals whose conduct is ethically positive are happier and more satisfied than those who neglect ethics.

—His Holiness the Fourteenth Dalai Lama

Raising a child to tell the truth (and tell it quickly) as well as make ethical choices empowers him or her. This type of power within allows a child to say "I may have to stand alone in protecting the bullied kid on the playground, but I am going to do it." Or "If the whole class is cheating on the spelling exam, but I realize that it isn't a smart choice and will only cause me unhappiness, then I will not cheat."

Honest children also come to rely upon themselves and develop a sense of self-trust that is essential to inner confidence. These kids aren't perfect kids either—they are just learning how to make choices in the world that honor who they are and where they want to go. They aren't trying to "get one over" on someone else—they are studying for their exams and doing the best they can. Boys and girls like this are learning how to be truthful even in tough moments, and they are learning to make ethical choices instead of living in fear of getting caught cheating, stealing, or lying. That's a big step toward building self-trust and developing a deeper belief in one's self.

One of the biggest lessons I teach children is the Golden Rule since it helps them make honest and moral choices. The idea is that what you give out will get returned to you. It's the law of cause and effect. When I discuss this idea, one of the questions I ask young children is, "If you are in school and you take someone else's pencil, is that stealing?" Most children say no. But when I explain that stealing is taking anything that isn't offered to you from anyone, their eyes open up wide.

I further explain that if you take a pencil from someone else that hasn't been given to you, then when you need a pencil there is a good chance that you won't be able to find one, because someone will have taken yours. The lesson here is if you take something or steal, someone will likely steal from you. If you lie, someone will likely lie to you. And so on.

This example (even though it is oversimplified) helps a child gain the basis for a profound understanding of the law of causality (Karma in Buddhism). What you give out gets returned to you like a boomerang.

Being the most honest version of yourself sets a good example for your child to develop the habit of honesty and positive ethical conduct. So do you pretend not to be home when you are? Do you return the excess money the clerk gave you by accident? Do you tell the truth when someone asks, "How are you?" Answer these in the privacy of your mind. If you believe you can be a wee bit more honest, make the decision to do it now, and set that positive example for your child. And in my experience, the more honest you are, the bigger gifts the Universe will bestow on you and the happier you naturally become.

Compassion

> *In separateness lies the world's great misery,*
> *in compassion lays the world's true strength.*
>
> —Buddha

Cultivating compassion in children gives them the personal experience of feeling connected to others, and often this will move them into action. Donating toys, walking your elderly neighbor's dog, or carrying a friend's backpack while he is on crutches empowers your child. Seeing their actions as impactful increases their growing sense of inner confidence.

Recently, I read a very compelling story of two boys who learned compassion from their parents and are bringing it powerfully into the world. Their names are Craig and Marc Keilburger, the founders of a charitable organization called Free the Children (www.freethe children.org). In their book *The World Needs Your Kid*, they share some of the amazing things their parents did to cultivate compassion:

• When the boys had birthday parties, their mom encouraged them to invite the kids others might exclude—in other words, they learned to include instead of exclude others.

- Dad's daily newspaper was used to discuss what was going on in the world from the perspective of "What can I do about it?" Morning became a time to connect about life and what the family could do to make it work for more people.

- The boys' parents modeled compassion by inviting people who didn't have any family or anywhere else to go to join the Keilburgers for Thanksgiving dinner.

- Both parents shared their previous experiences with making the world a better place. Mom worked with the homeless and Dad volunteered with the mentally disabled. Each parent shared not just what they did, but why, and how it made them feel. In other words, they explained how each action built their confidence that they could make a difference, and these stories planted the seed in their children.

- As parents, this couple also stayed engaged in what was really going on in their sons' lives. If they heard of a bullying episode, they would ask who did the bullying and what did the boys do—or not do? They wanted Marc and Craig to understand that they weren't off the hook just because they weren't bullies themselves.

- The boys' mom and dad also encouraged their activism. For example, Marc was upset as a child when he found out a housing development was going to be built over a pond where the boys found tadpoles in the summer and went ice skating in the winter. In response, the parents didn't just commiserate about the loss. They empowered their son to write a few words on a piece of paper and have all the neighbors sign it. This was his first petition to city hall.

Both of these boys credit their compassion and desire to make the world a better place completely to their parents. They learned to think of others, wondered what it was like in their "shoes," and looked at the world as one big place where they could have a positive impact. They continue to do so through their nonprofit organization, Free the Children. Marc said, "Mom and Dad laid the groundwork by ensuring we contributed to the family, the neighborhood, and our school."

So when you focus on fostering compassion, your child will be inspired to take actions that make the world a bit better for themselves and others. This activity strengthens their growing sense of inner confidence.

Wisdom

Knowing others is intelligence; knowing yourself is true wisdom. Mastering others is strength; mastering yourself is true power.

—Lao Tzu, Taoist philosopher

Connecting to wisdom is essential for the deepening of inner confidence. Children who just believe they are strong but cannot ground this "knowing" in a story from their culture or spiritual tradition are floating on the ocean without an anchor. Once dropped, the anchor keeps them steady. An example is the Buddhist "Precious Human Life" story that stabilizes in a child how fortunate he or she is to have this human life and what it naturally bestows on him or her. It describes the advanced consciousness of a human, how rare it is to get a birth as a human (not a turtle or toad), and how in this very lifetime you can achieve lasting happiness for the benefit of yourself and others. (See the full story in Chapter 8.)

Wisdom traditions help children learn over and over again to deeper degrees throughout their lives why they are powerful creators. Jesus, the master teacher, said, "Behold, the Kingdom of God is within you" and that resonates with me. This is the idea that within each of us is the power of all there is, something we need to remind ourselves on a daily basis and help our children see, too.

Applying wisdom to your everyday life is the only way inner confidence can happen. You needn't be spiritual or religious—just connect with ideas that empower your conception of yourself as powerful and spark that in your children. Wisdom teachers have emerged in nearly every tradition; some contemporary ones are Esther Hicks channeling Abraham, and Michael Bernard Beckwith.

Anthropologist Jane Goodall explained, "My mother encouraged me and told me I could make my dreams reality if I worked hard and believed in myself." Jane's mother taught her that believing in herself was a "key" to making her dreams come true. This is wisdom. Another wise piece of advice I heard my parent client, Martha, give her seven-year-old daughter is: "Sweetheart, every morning we say mottos together so we can have the best day ever!" This is wisdom, too. Because every parent and child needs to steer their mind into positive, empowering places so that life works easier.

Connecting your child to wisdom helps anchor within him or her a deeper belief in his or her positive sense of self that can deepen over a lifetime.

Back to the Blocks

The Five Building Blocks of Confidence provides a framework for you to create this deeper sense of confidence in your children. Buddhist concepts of ethical discipline, compassion in action, and wisdom also fit nicely into this model.

For example, my neighbor's son Jack discovered a baby crow that was injured after falling out of her nest. He wanted her to stop suffering (Block Two: Beliefs) and also felt terrible looking at her all alone on the lawn (Block Three: Emotions). Jack knocked on my door for help, and together we called the animal rescue center to see what they could do. This was compassion in action.

Of course, the more your children "hang around" with other compassionate children (Block Four: Social), the more those thoughts are supported by others, too.

Inner Confidence: The Plan for Life

Chances are good that you have guided your child to that deeper sense of confidence after they have come home feeling shaken, uncertain, or insecure. Since childhood is full of bumps—whether they are a broken bone, a bully on the bus, or a failed spelling exam—everything can be used as fodder to create inner confidence.

The Three-Step Process shared in this chapter is one more tool in your parenting toolbox so you can effectively lead your child toward his or her most empowering life.

Along with supporting your child's deeper sense of confidence, you gained a sense of how some children need extra help in cultivating confidence. There's nothing wrong with these kids and actually there is so much RIGHT with these children—they solely need skillful assistance so they can let go of any limitations in their thinking and learn how to embrace themselves as the powerful creators they are today.

The Five Building Blocks of Confidence remains the one proven system for cultivating inner confidence in children. Buddhism emphasizes cultivating ethics, compassion, and wisdom—which also fit nicely into this framework as cultivating inner confidence—so I shared them here, too.

Next up, we look at creative and scientifically proven ways to build self-confidence in your children every single day.

Buckle up!

8

The Inner Confidence Plan for Life

Without a humble but reasonable confidence
in your own powers you cannot be successful or happy.

—Norman Vincent Peale

Becoming a parent who is able to believe in one's self and be the bridge to help your children believe in themselves, too—this is successful parenting. Until now, the process of how to develop that deeper belief in one's self has been mysterious at best. Suggestions have ranged from getting hypnotized to wearing particular colors that bolster self-confidence. These methods may be helpful, but they only addressed a piece of the confidence puzzle.

The Five Building Blocks of Confidence shared in this book is a holistic program encapsulating the central pieces of the confidence puzzle. From optimizing your child's physical health to guiding you to help your child think inwardly confident thoughts, this system is using a mind, body, and spirit approach to nurturing your child's overall sense of inner confidence.

Confidence Habits

Biology: The foundational Building Block of Confidence.

- **Eat healthy:** Look for ways to improve your child's diet, whether it's adding a protein shake, chewable vitamins, or more leafy green vegetables.

- **Exercise:** How much physical exercise does your child get? If she needs more, seek fun and easy ways to increase her activity that she'll enjoy, like team sports or a new trampoline.

- **Sleep well:** Ensure your child gets a consistent level of sleep nightly for optimum brain development.

Beliefs: The creator Building Block of Confidence.

- **Connect to wisdom:** Consciously expose your child's mind to a philosophy or way of thinking that empowers him or her. It may be sharing a spiritual tradition, like Buddhism, or contemporary new age thinking as taught by well-regarded teachers like Louise Hay and Michael Bernard Beckwith.

- **Think confident thoughts:** Be a role model of inwardly confident thoughts and teach your child how to think these thoughts, too.

- **Create a daily practice:** Practice "training" your child's mind so that he'll see himself as powerful and capable every day.

Emotions: The intensifier Building Block of Confidence.

- **Feel confidence:** Give your child opportunities to feel confident and help him or her remember that feeling inside—that he or she can do anything!

- **Ground it in the body:** Use movement like Yoga, stretching, or balance exercises to guide your child to feel the inner strength inside of him or her.

- **Remember that when you think confident thoughts, the feelings follow:** Teach your child that his or her thoughts will directly create his or her feelings.

Social: The strengthener Building Block of Confidence.

- **Positive self-talk:** Create a fun, regular practice of reciting positive sayings that plant the seed of self-confidence in your child.

- **Create an uplifting community:** Appreciate the uplifting people in your child's life, from teachers to coaches. Does he or she need more supportive people around or fewer draining influences?

- **Design an uplifting space:** Make your child's bedroom or special corner in the home somewhere that lifts him or her up inwardly (for example, place certificates, photos of special moments, trophies, and pictures of inner dreams up in this space).

Spiritual: The expander Building Block of Confidence.

- **Believe in something greater:** Introduce your child to God, Spirit, Source, Nature, or whatever you believe is the infinite power of the Universe.

- **Recognize that this greater power is in you and your child:** Lead your child to understand that this infinite power, greatness, and "God Stuff" is within him or her.

- **Live from this place:** Practice living every day from the awareness that each of us has great power within us now. Teach this awareness to your child on a day-by-day basis.

As you likely recall, the last two chapters guided you on how to help your child regain his or her confidence after it has been shaken. This process of helping your child course-correct and get back on the path of inner confidence is essential; life has this funny way of serving bumps, whether it is a "friend" who says something mean or failing an exam after studying so hard.

But as you guide your child to that deeper place of confidence, there is something mysterious that will happen—you will both feel happier, too. You won't get hooked on believing that you can't do something or that some obstacle is greater than you are. This type of happiness stems from the knowing that you are capable, talented, and powerful right now to succeed no matter what.

Therefore, confidence comes before happiness. And inner confidence is a prerequisite for lasting happiness. And that is every parent's deepest wish—to raise a happy child.

So to help you with that goal, this chapter focuses on making your life easier and sharing proven exercises that foster inner confidence. Confidence like this will serve your children their entire lives and help them become happier day by day.

As you have learned, creating confidence takes practice; it takes repeated actions to create new neural pathways in the brain that support a deeper level of confidence. Here are three guiding principles to help you on the way:

✓ Connect with empowering ideas.

✓ Find fun ways to "remind" your child of these every day.

✓ Surround your kids with people, places, and things that lift them UP.

Connect with Empowering Ideas

Throughout this book, I've described the importance of connecting to empowering ideas. The ideas don't need to be spiritual or religious; use whatever helps your child understand that power is within him or her.

My brand of empowering ideas is rooted in Buddhism, although it's influenced by my Roman Catholic background and my contemporary studies with modern-day teachers like Louise Hay, Caroline Myss, Doreen Virtue, and Wayne Dyer. Both Dyer and Virtue have written children's books that also convey such wisdom: *Thank You, Angels!* by Virtue and *Incredible You!* by Dyer.

These ideas resonate deeply with me, but I understand that they may not be your cup of tea. Your role is to connect with the empowering ideas that lift you up and share those heartfelt messages with your children to empower them, too.

Everyday Empowerment

After connecting with the ideas that empower your child, you need to remind him or her of those ideas every single day. These repeated actions are what pave their new pathways in the brain to support inner confidence. Of course, just connecting with wisdom or empowering ideas on a daily basis isn't enough: you also need to make the connecting enjoyable.

As I shared earlier, I sit in the silence (meditate) and then speak my affirmations every morning to open the way for a positive day. During my family breakfast routine, I also love to play uplifting music like Denise Hagan's songs "For Those Who Hear" and "I Am Everything" that genuinely uplift my mind, body, and spirit.

I also suggest using the car ride to school as the perfect place (they're captive!) to lean your child's mind toward confident thoughts and feeling those confident feelings. Perhaps you are even more awake and focused in the evening, so bedtime may be a better place to carve a few minutes to seed inner confidence.

However you help your children think those amazing thoughts of their power, the important thing to remember is to help them do it with feeling on a *daily basis*.

Empowering All Around

Creating a sense of inner confidence in children means they are not just learning it from you. You have surrounded them with the people, places, and things that consistently serve to bolster their growing sense of self-confidence.

Although it was decades ago, I remember a bright spot when I was in fifth grade, where my confidence got uplifted weekly at Girl Scouts. I learned how to handle money, sell cookies, become responsible for myself, and master other tasks like building a campfire with assistance. My troop leader (name long forgotten but feeling remembered) always encouraged us to believe in ourselves and have the courage to be ourselves. This regular afterschool activity served as a way to increase my sense of self-confidence. (I am sure you also recognize it as an outer confidence feedback loop, too.)

All children—no matter how smart, skilled, and capable they are—benefit from the experience of having people around them to nudge them forward on the path toward inner confidence. This support may take many forms, from a fantastic soccer coach to finding "just the right school" that helps your child see his or her strength, power, and talents on a daily basis. The idea is that your children will become what they surround themselves with—so be sure to put the most inwardly confident people, places, and things near them.

Confidence Exercises

Now that you know the three guiding principles (they are almost like the *Cliffs Notes* of confidence), you can pick and choose the types of regular activities you'll use to cultivate this growing sense of strength in your children. Of course, the aim continues to be to help our children get to know inner confidence in their own minds, bodies, and spirits.

Here are some confidence-building activities to choose from as you create your daily program of nurturing confidence in yourself and your child.

Prayer

Spiritual practice brings both long-term
happiness and more inner strength day by day.

—His Holiness the Fourteenth Dalai Lama

Prayer is one of the most effective ways to create a daily practice that focuses your mind, lifts your spirit, and reminds your child of his or her greatness. Some children will naturally be drawn to the side of life that is invisible, metaphysical, and spiritual in nature. These children are ideal candidates for using prayer as a primary method to remind them of their infinite power on a daily basis.

Some prayers that spark a deeper sense of awareness of my divinity, infinite power, and greatness within are the following:

Buddhist

"A Precious Human Life" by *His Holiness the Fourteenth Dalai Lama*

Every day, think as you wake up,
Today I am fortunate to have woken up,
I am alive, I have a precious human life,
I am not going to waste it
I am going to use
All my energies to develop myself.
To expand my heart out to others,
To achieve enlightenment for
The benefit of all beings,
I am going to have kind
Thoughts towards others,
I am not going to get angry,
Or think badly about others,
I am going to benefit others
As much as I can.

Interfaith

"Today" by *Maureen Healy*

Today is a great day.
I have a strong heart
And happy mind.
May I look to others
with a smile and
offer a helping hand.
May I laugh and play
and accept all the
good coming my way.

Christian

"Good Morning, God" by *Maureen Healy*

Good Morning, God.
I know today is great.
You'll stay with me
Inside my heart
Helping me be strong
All day long.
You lift me up
When I feel stinky
showing me the way
Each and every day.

Nondenominational

"Prayer for Peace" by *Mahatma Gandhi*

I offer you peace.
I offer you love.
I offer you friendship.
I see your beauty.
I hear your need.
I feel your feelings.
My wisdom flows from
the Highest Source.
I salute that Source in you.
Let us work together
for unity and love.

Within each prayer, several things are happening: First, you and your child recognize you are strong; second, you acknowledge that this strength is within you and isn't going anywhere; third, you will rely on this power within to help you.

One of my parent clients, Maria, started praying with her two children every morning, using prayers that reflect her family as powerful, creative, and strong. After a few weeks, she wrote me a note: "Maureen, thank you so much. I always thought of prayer as asking God for what I wanted or thanking Him for things. You helped me see it differently—now I can say a prayer with my kids to strengthen them for the day. I love it!"

Affirmations

You have power over your mind—not outside events.
Realize this, and you will find strength.

—Marcus Aurelius, Roman emperor and philosopher

Like adults, children need to get into the habit of speaking to themselves positively, repetitively, and with great feeling so they can convince both the conscious and subconscious mind that they are completely capable and can succeed in life.

This positive self-talk—which you can practice every day with affirmations—actually rewires the brain and steers it in a confident direction. From research into the biology of thinking, we know that if you change your thinking, you can literally change your brain—and ultimately change your life.

Denis Waitley, a motivational speaker featured in the popular film *The Secret*, suggests the most important key to the permanent enhancement of self-esteem is positive self-talk. (I'd replace "self-esteem" with the word "confidence.") Saying daily affirmations and teaching your child how to say "confidence-building" ones with feeling can seed inner confidence.

Here are some key tips to help your child use daily affirmations:

• Keep them simple
• Use those that "spark" your child's feelings
• Create them together
• Involve as many senses as possible

By giving your children simple sayings that they can use whenever they want, you are empowering them and giving them the message that they can begin steering their own emotional boat instead of just reacting to the choppy waters. This message may sound simple, but it's actually quite sophisticated. The saying must also be felt to be effective; it must be simple so your child recalls it when he or she needs it most. If the affirmation involves more than one of the senses, chances are that it will be easier to remember.

For example, my client Nancy is a very visual child. To help her recall her favorite daily confidence-building motto, she painted it on the mirror in her bedroom. Each morning before second grade, she looks in her mirror and repeats her motto. Her mother reports that it helps Nancy feel "super great." The daily dose of uplifting and strengthening sayings has helped Nancy become more sure of herself and confident in new situations.

Please use these sayings as starting points. You may use them verbatim, or they may spark your original creations. Let them be what they need to be. These sayings have been extraordinarily helpful for my child clients around the world:

Confidence-Building Sayings

- I am awesome in every way.
- Within me is the same power that holds the stars in the sky.
- I have God inside. God is unbeatable. So I am unbeatable.
- I am strong [put hand on heart].
- I can do it.
- Inside of me is pure positive energy.
- I am made of "God Stuff" that makes me tough.
- I love life, and life loves all of me.

These confidence-building sayings were created especially for kids. They're simple, but with repetition, they've had a profound impact on helping kids see themselves as being highly capable to master tasks and persevere in life (self-confidence). Kids will also feel better about themselves (self-esteem), too.

Meditation

Meditation brings wisdom; lack of meditation leaves ignorance.
Know well what leads you forward and what
holds you back, and choose the path that leads to wisdom.

—Buddha

Children's minds can calm down through meditation. Children who have learned how to reduce their "monkey mind" have stronger mental faculties—they can direct their minds consciously toward positive and empowering ideas. The child who learns how to steer his or her thoughts toward inner confidence can overcome any obstacle and learn how to be happier.

I work with meditation in the two primary ways that are taught in my Tibetan Buddhist tradition:

- **Placement**—Most people use the word "meditation" to refer to the practice of focusing on one thing like the breath, looking at a candle, or being led in a guided visualization to achieve a certain objective (for example, increased calmness, inner peace, clarity, compassion, and confidence). This type of meditation is rooted in experience: through your experience, these results might occur.

- **Analytical**—This type of meditation is also about focusing on one thing but less from an experiential standpoint and more from reason. Hearing His Holiness the Dalai Lama or Lama Surya Das talk about

confidence would be considered a teaching or analytical meditation on
the subject matter. It is rooted in reason: Through your thinking mind,
you come to a logical conclusion on a topic.

Both types of meditation are valid ways to plant the seeds of inner
confidence. My preference is to begin with a placement meditation—
it may be a breathing exercise or guided meditation like visualization,
so children can calm their mind and also learn how to experience
their power within (either feeling or imagining).

Try analytical meditation when your children can really consider an
idea and engage in a discussion. The discussion or talk can be simple:
you're merely seeking to plant the seeds of inner confidence, perhaps
discuss where true power comes from (wink, wink—inside), and really
help them see themselves as powerful, capable, and with great potential.

To help you get started, I am providing two sample meditations
below. The first one is a guided meditation designed to help your
child connect with his or her source of power inside (placement).
The second meditation is the story of a "Precious Human Life" about
how every person is full of great potential, power, and capability
right now (analytical meditation).

Meditation (Visualization)
(To be read aloud by an adult)

*Get comfortable and really relaxed, whether it's sitting up in a chair
with your feet touching the floor or laying down in your bed. The important thing is to feel awake and ready to imagine.*

*Close your eyes. Imagine that you're sitting on a rock in your favorite
place. You are on this rock, and it's the perfect time of day: The sun is
golden and the wind is cool; a perfect breeze is flowing; and you're just
so happy to be there. Blue birds are chirping, hummingbirds are zoom-*

ing around, and doves are gently sitting beside you.

All of a sudden, you're joined on this rock by your Guardian Angel. She wants to tell you something very important. She says, "Within you is the POWER to do, be, or have anything in the whole world. You can feel this power by breathing slowly and remembering that you have the God Spark* within you. So put your hand on your heart, and feel yourself breathing in and out. Do this and feel your power for a few moments.

[Pause while child learns to focus on breathing in, breathing out, and being calm.]

Your Guardian Angel now wants to also give you something. She taps your right shoulder and gives you wings. She says, "Dear One, you are a Divine Being that has come to this time and space for great reason. You came only to be YOU. So enjoy fully and completely being you. Human eyes cannot see your wings, but I promise you, they are always there. . . .

Any time you need to feel strong, you can always put your hand on your heart, breathe in your strength, and picture your wings. With just a few deep breaths, you will immediately feel strong because both you and I know the truth: that you are powerful beyond words and have come from Spirit to play on Planet Earth.

Our time today is almost up, but you can call on me anytime, and I will send you strength and help. Whenever you need a little extra Angel support from up above, we'll help you and send some love. But also remember: you can feel strong by placing your hand on your heart, taking a few deep breaths, and remembering yourself as the powerful being that you are."

Your Guardian Angel must go now. She wants you to know that anytime you need her help just call her name—either out loud or in your mind—and she'll immediately come to help you feel more calm, stronger, and loved instantly.

It's now time to come back to the room. Move your fingers, take some deep breaths, and begin to open your eyes.

*Note: Substitute Spirit, Source, Buddha Seed, Christ—whatever you prefer.

You can inquire about this process and discuss it with your child: How did it feel to him or her? If it seems right, you can suggest children begin using their imaginations on their own whenever they need to feel strong.

Meditation ("Precious Human Life")
(To be read aloud by an adult)

Once upon a time, 2,500 years ago, a man named Siddhartha Gautama walked the Earth. He was born of a noble family, and he was a prince. One day, he decided to leave his life of riches and help people become free from the pain of everyday living. He wanted everyone to be happy, feel great joy, and be free from pain.

So he traveled across his country of India, in Asia, and studied with spiritual teachers. He learned how to meditate. One day, meditating under a bodhi tree in Bodhi Gaya, he reached a clear state of mind, free from confusion: He became "awakened" to the truths of this world. Since that day and that moment of enlightenment, Siddhartha became known as the "Buddha," or "awakened one."

Buddha's disciples and the king, Brahma, requested that he share what he had learned. Buddha wanted people to understand how precious it was to be born a human. He gathered his students and said:

"Welcome. I am the Buddha, and you have received a precious human life. The chances of getting a human life are so rare—only once in a million eons would the stars align and you would have the great fortune of being born a human. You see, I believe that you had the possibility of being born a humpback whale, or mosquito, or many other things. Being born a human is one of the most rare and precious gifts you could receive.

As a human, you have advanced mental capabilities and great potential within you to become happy and live the life of your dreams. This life brings your talents into this world and calls you to be the best of yourself—helping others and realizing that you are connected to everyone. It is important that you begin seeing yourself as talented and capable, because this will help you have the courage and confidence to be fully you. This world needs you to be fully you and only you—so you get to bring your unique gifts to this planet."

Buddha finished his talk about how rare and special a human life is. He decided to call this gift of being born a human a "treasure"—like a precious gem.

Of course, these aren't the only meditations that you can use to build your child's understanding and direct experience of their power—they are just a starting point. So my suggestion is to continue your discovery of using meditation as a method to empower yourself and your family to lead your best lives.

Music

Music is the language of the spirit. It opens
the secret of life bringing peace, and abolishing strife.

—Kahlil Gibran, author of *The Prophet*

Songs sometimes find their way into a child's heart even faster than words. For this reason, I love playing uplifting music that helps children focus on their good and claim their power in playful yet purposeful ways. I play music every day during shower time or breakfast to get everyone going on the right note.

One of my favorite songs of late is Denise Hagan's "Perfect Replications," which she received in a dream from the master teacher, Jesus Christ. Here are some of the lyrics:

If you could see
what I see
You'd lose your
breath for sure.
You are the
perfect replications
And the ones that
I adore.
I carved you from
the diamonds
And polished you
with love.
And I sent you
out beyond the veil
so you might
choose the love.
Oh, my sweet creations
Your beauty makes me weak.
Oh, my sweet creations
The whole world's at your feet.
And one day soon
you'll see it.
If you could see what I see,
you'd never lose your smile.
You walk in my own footsteps
When you walk that second mile.
These are more than words, my love.
This is poetry divine.
My signature is everywhere
For all of life is mine.

One day you'll see what I see,
And you'll come to realize
Every tear you ever cried
I wiped from my own eyes.
I know your every feeling,
And I have felt your every joy.
But you and I are one my child
Still illusion is the choice.

Another positive and uplifting song is Francine Jarry's "Joy, Joy, Joy" (found on the Abraham Hicks' website, www.abraham-hicks.com). Here are some of the lyrics:

Dream big, I can do it.
I can do it, I can do it, I can do it.
Feel good, I can do it.
I can do it, I can do it, I can do it.

Joy, joy, joy! It's all there for me.
Joy, joy, joy! Joy is the key!

Be well, I can do it.
I can do it, I can do it, I can do it.
Have fun, I can do it.
I can do it, I can do it, I can do it.

One song that I have used exclusively with children to bolster inner confidence is "Gotta Be Me" by Secret Agent 23 Skidoo (www.secretagent23skidoo.com). Here are some of their lyrics:

There's a whole lotta people
all across the world

a whole lotta boys
a whole lotta girls
a whole lotta
fathers and uncles and brothers
a whole lotta
sisters and aunts and mothers
and whether they're parents
or whether they're children
every single one of them's
a little bit different
there's only one thing that
makes us the same
we all got our own face
we all got our own name
we all got our own brain
we all got our own style
what's style? well, that's
the way that you smile
and the way that you walk
and the way that you talk
and the way that you look
from your hat to your socks
it's a beautiful thing
being yourself
and not trying to act like
everyone else
I'm a tell you the truth
and you gotta agree
man, I can't be you, nope
I gotta be me

So enjoy empowering your child through the beauty of music. Through listening or creating something together with drums, guitars, homemade shakers, cymbals, or whatever instruments you can gather, music will add to your child's sense of confidence.

Movement

To keep the body in good health is a duty, otherwise
we shall not be able to keep our mind strong and clear.

—Buddha

Along with saying affirmations, singing songs, or listening to music, movement can be a way to create everyday empowerment. I once worked with a single mother who loved practicing Yoga as a way to relax and feel stronger. She took great pride in her morning sun salutations, and I suggested that she begin including her daughter, who immediately connected with the practice.

The exercises suggested here will strengthen your child's growing sense of personal power that is located in his or her third chakra—the seat of inner confidence. *Chakra* is a Sanskrit term meaning wheel; many ancient traditions believe that we have energetic "wheels" associated with different life functions like survival, creativity, communication, love, and so on. Each of the seven primary wheels correlates to a place in the body; the third chakra is in the stomach area. So when I talk about feeling strong from the inside out, there's actually a correlated physical and energetic place where this occurs: the core of a child (stomach area) feels stronger, radiating strength from the inside out.

Some types of exercise designed to strengthen a child from the inside out include:

- **Yoga**. The word "yoga" in Sanskrit means "union of the body and mind." These exercises are designed to clear the mind, strengthen the body, and uplift the spirit. Some yoga poses specifically designed to strengthen confidence include: Archer, Tree, Superman, and Child's pose. Martha Wenig, founder of YogaKids, also authored a popular book on the subject titled *YogaKids: Educating the Whole Child through Yoga* that you may find helpful.

- **Tai Chi Chuan.** Tai Chi is a form of slow physical movement that uses one's inner strength as its force. Even though there's little to no physical contact with others, it's considered great physical exercise and martial arts therapy. Studies suggest it can increase a child's ability to focus and provide mental calmness.

- **Karate.** Karate is a form of higher-impact physical movement that is practiced as a form of self-defense and a sport. Many kids begin karate because it looks cool, but soon they become students of its philosophy that teaches focus and mental power to overcome your opponent; it also emphasizes cultivating inner strength.

- **Parkour.** Parkour is a method of movement that focuses on efficiency and speed while moving around obstacles. It has become very popular with children in the United States, since it draws from the worlds of gymnastics and martial arts. Through training, it's believed that kids learn how to overcome not only physical but emotional and mental obstacles, too.

The type of exercise chosen isn't a big deal; what's more important is to keep nudging your child to think confident thoughts, feel those feelings, and anchor that experience into his or her body.

Children who are mentally, emotionally, and physically strong are also "bully-proofing" themselves for their school years. I promise you this isn't a small point to be made—bullying can destroy a child's growing sense of confidence.

Mindfulness

> *The most precious gift we can offer anyone*
> *is our attention. When mindfulness embraces*
> *those we love, they bloom like flowers.*
>
> —Thich Nhat Hanh

Children who practice mindfulness are able to take a "sacred pause" and make a conscious choice from an empowered place. They are learning not to be swept away by negative thoughts or emotions but to stop and reconnect to themselves—their power, truth, strength—then go forward in that moment knowing who they are.

One of my child clients, Morgan, at nine years old was very stressed about her upcoming end-of-grade exams. "I just freeze when I sit down to take a test," said Morgan. (I didn't tell her but I did the same thing at her age.) Understanding her fear, I helped her learn how to "pause" when she felt wobbly—this pause is where mindfulness is growing—then we together created a saying that worked for Morgan to "click" her back into a mindset of strength, confidence, and greater ease for successful exam completion. Her saying was: "I am superhero smart, and these tests are easy for me!" She then used it before (and during) the exams, and the great news is it worked—all tests were passed.

Mindfulness is the ability to pay greater attention in the present moment and learn how to see life more clearly. My work with Morgan was focused on helping her to recognize herself as highly capable and "seeing" that clearly instead of letting her fear, anxiety, and limited thinking overshadow her life experience. She is an incredibly talented, capable, and creative child, but in order for her to develop inner confidence, she needs to learn how to apply antidotes to her fear when it comes up. This begins with becoming aware of what is happening when it is happening so she can learn to consciously move toward what she wants.

Other moments that mindfulness is extremely helpful for children, especially as it relates to their development of inner confidence, are:

- Rejection   (Peer rejection, teasing, bullying, sibling conflict)
- Failure   (Failed a test)
- Stress   (Busy schedules, high pressure to perform
                 well, family stress)
- Sadness   (Experiencing loss, disappointment)
- Doubt   (Highly critical of self, has perfectionistic tendencies)

Because in these moments, I have found that children who can metaphorically "stop, drop, and roll" like the old Smokey Bear commercial are more successful in guiding themselves toward inner confidence. It is so easy to feel down, forget your power, see yourself as a failure, or begin creating negative confidence feedback loops. But the child who begins going off his or her confidence course and recognizes that can learn how to course-correct. This "seeing it" is the moment of mindfulness where children can begin again. They can learn how to let go of the failure, stress, sadness, or other way of seeing themselves as small and embrace themselves as bigger than anything in front of them.

Through my own practice of mindfulness, I have honed my ability to teach children to create that "sacred pause" in their own lives whether they are upset at school, on the bus, or playing in the backyard—they can stop and take a deep breath, remind themselves of their power, and then go forward without fear. I believe Thich Nhat Hanh captured this sentiment perfectly when he said:

> I am inviting you to go deeper, to learn and to practice so that you become someone who has a great capacity for being solid, calm, and without fear, because our society needs people like you who have these qualities, and your children, our children, need people like you, in order to go on, in order to become solid, and calm, and without fear.

Creative Arts

Creativity and artistic expression are great ways for children to claim their inner power, and technology can help:

- **Mind Movies.** These are videos that help adults and children manifest their dreams, whether the dream is for a new bicycle or for feeling happier. I suggest creating a "mind movie" with your child that focuses on helping him or her feel inwardly confident. Pepper it with affirmations, images of his or her success, and perhaps use a song in the video that really lifts his or her heart. For more information, check out www.mindmovies.com.

- **Creative Pictures.** Ask your child to draw himself or herself as "divine," then hang this image up. The more a child can see that "God Stuff" is within him or her, the easier it is to plant inner confidence. One of my former students, Hannah, drew an image of herself as the Buddha, with a rainbow above her and flowers sprinkled with glitter around her. (It was so beautiful!) Her mother told me, "Hannah smiles every morning as she awakes to her framed image of herself as a Buddha!"

• **Audio.** Whenever I go off my "inner confidence" course, I have an audio on my smartphone of a spiritual mind treatment (prayer) said by one of my teachers that "clicks" me back into place. It reminds me that God is everywhere and in everyone, and with that knowing, I can claim my power. (You might have a different audio inclination, but using a "reminder" audio for your son or daughter can be very effective.)

Children who split time between parents can benefit greatly from audio and video recordings. For example, the audio may be your voice reminding them that you love them, see them as powerful inside, and that your faith in them is unshakable. (You can also do this as an MP3 for an iPod or other recording device.) I love this choice because it empowers children: They can play the audio or video whenever they need to hear your voice and feel uplifted. The reality is we can't always be there.

These aren't the only suggestions, but I hope they'll provide you with a starting point to get your creative juices flowing with ways you can surround your child with "daily reminders" of his or her power.

Helping Hands

> *If you think you are too small*
> *to make a difference, try sleeping with a mosquito.*
>
> —African Proverb

One family I have worked closely with started a new practice: each morning, they go around the breakfast table and ask, "Who can I help today?" Their answers range from walking the family dog to praying for world peace. Amanda, the mother, loves this practice. "It got everyone focused on helping others and less about our own self-ish needs," she told me.

Compassionate acts seed inner strength and confidence. As children do "good things" and see that they have power now, their sense of inner confidence grows. These good things might be donating old books, giving to a charity like Child Fund International and getting a pen pal, doing a loving-kindness meditation, taking up a cause like recycling, or making visits to your local nursing home in a clown costume just to cheer people up. The point is that children have great power right now. If you connect children to something that sparks their interest, cultivates the belief that they can make little contributions now, and become part of the growing solution, they will begin developing a deeper sense of confidence in themselves. And if children are thinking on a much larger scale, your assistance may be needed as they venture into helping others around the globe.

I recently helped landscape a new Habitat for Humanity home in North Carolina. I love the outdoors, so I enjoyed raking, planting trees, moving dirt, and creating flower beds. I delighted in the feeling of helping and working together with others to make an immediate difference for a new family's home. Plus, I felt really powerful that my hands helped to make a happier home for someone—I know the kids who joined in felt it, too.

The Dynamic Process

Sparking your child's sense of inner confidence will happen in many ways over time. Your son might love doing affirmations as a family until he turns seven, and then he loses interest in the idea of "sayings time"; at that point, you can shift toward creating uplifting movies with him and strengthening his positive sense of self through music.

The more your child participates in these activities, the faster he or she is paving new pathways in his or her brain for inner confidence to take hold. This is also a positive confidence feedback loop that strengthens your child's growing sense of self-confidence.

Ultimately, the creation of inner confidence is about plugging into the Five Building Blocks of Confidence and making them come alive for your family. The practice will certainly change as your children grow, but the thread throughout is that you're planting the seeds of this deeper belief in themselves and helping them "see" themselves as powerful, creative, and highly capable today.

Be Part of the Confidence Revolution

As you animate the Five Building Blocks of Confidence in your family's life, it won't be hard to find others to join you—there's a genuine confidence revolution going on. It is showing up everywhere in books, television programs, radio shows, children's toys, and professional conferences; it seems that almost everyone wants to be sure that more children grow up strong from the inside out.

Confidence as a subject has grabbed people's interest, but along with it is also the big topic of happiness. Happiness is the gold prize that every parent wants to experience and also to nurture in their children. In this book, we discussed the connection between inner confidence and lasting happiness, so that more parents and children can become stronger and go for the gold.

So the attainment of inner confidence, and, ultimately, happiness is about shifting the way we empower our children. Instead of just saying "great job" when they earn a 100 percent on a spelling test, we help children believe in themselves before the outer world can show them they are great.

Being a parent who is in alignment with the deeper truth of your child as someone who came here with power, capabilities, and great potential—this puts you as a leading-edge parent, a parent who knows your child's power from the get-go and encourages him or her to be the person he or she came here to be.

Parenting with this knowing and nurturing that deeper belief in your child is captured perfectly by the words of motivational speaker Brian Tracy:

> If you raise your children to feel that they can accomplish any goal or task they decide upon, you will have succeeded as a parent, and you will have given your children the greatest of all blessings.

Inner Confidence: My Personal Journey

In the Introduction, I shared some of my journey moving from outer confidence to inner confidence. This journey was a physical one, where I brought me, myself, and I with backpacks galore to the base of the Himalayas to study with happiness and confidence masters. Little did I know that this physical journey really turned into a mental and emotional one, where everything in my way was fodder for inner confidence—the freezing temperatures, weekly showers out of a bucket, and transportation rides on the top of a bus!

Honestly, I am convinced that I really needed to sit on cushions at the seat of people who have been deemed enlightened beings so I could soak up what inner confidence really was.

Since I have been back in the United States, my life has more meaning. I realize at an even deeper level how important sharing the concepts of inner confidence is with you, parents raising children. Devoting a year of my life to writing this book has been gratifying;

interviewing parents around the globe, speaking with children who have ratcheted up their level of confidence, and continuing to serve a busy practice have been challenging things to accomplish at the same time. Things haven't been boring!

Caroline Myss explained when she wrote her book, *Sacred Contracts,* that books have their own energy. I agree fully, since the energy of inner confidence, strength, and power has pervaded my every turn this past year. I have been given countless opportunities to demonstrate my level of inner confidence—from being rushed to the hospital to helping neighbors who lost heat in the middle of winter. Universal forces seemed to be at play to help me know the concepts of inner confidence on the deepest level, and here I am—stronger and happier because of it.

My deepest wish for you and your children is that you let the wisdom of the world fill you up and bring you to a place of unremitting faith in yourselves. And as my mother used to say, "Keep the faith," because it is with faith that all things are possible.

Giving Back

In the spirit of giving back, Maureen is delighted to donate a portion of the author proceeds from *Growing Happy Kids* to the following two worthy causes:

UNICEF

This international organization provides humanitarian relief to children in over 150 countries. Many children continue to need basic medical care, clean drinking water, access to education (school in a box), emergency relief, and more assistance that UNICEF provides. Maureen feels particularly connected to UNICEF since the land and housing for her first Buddhist Center was donated by Maurice Pate, the cofounder of UNICEF, and provided her a place to learn about happiness that was free of charge. More information:

> United States Fund for UNICEF
> Maiden Lane
> New York, NY 10038
> 1-800-FOR-KIDS
> www.unicefusa.org or internationally: www.unicef.org

Seramey Thewo Khamtsen Children's Program

This donation provides basic supplies to young monastic students in Bylakuppe, India. Sera Mey Monastery was reestablished in India after His Holiness the Fourteenth Dalai Lama fled Tibet in 1959. Today, this location provides enormous benefit to the world through training young children in the method and wisdom of Tibetan Buddhism for the benefit of all sentient beings. It is only through supporting such a grassroots program does the ancient culture of Tibet get to continue to "pass on" their wisdom throughout the world. More information:

Do Ngak Kunphen Ling
(Program Administrators)
30 Putnam Park Road
Redding, CT 06896
info@dnkldharma.org

Acknowledgments

Thank you to my teachers. In this lifetime, I have had the great fortune of learning from authentic teachers in the Tibetan Buddhist tradition. Along with these masters, I have also been blessed to learn from spiritual teachers from multiple traditions such as New Thought and New Age.

In addition, I want to acknowledge my clients—those who came in small bodies and those who came in big ones. I have learned so much from each of you.

Specific thanks also goes to: Barbara and John Waterhouse, Christy Corna, Venerable Geshe Tashi, Venerable Geshe Lobsang Dhargye, Cynthia Andros, Steve Scott, Kathy Eldon, Lama Surya Das, Sharon Salzberg, Francine Jarry, Denise Hagan, Secret Agent 23 Skidoo, Mary Fox Kane, Jerry Rosa, Conor Rosa, Lynn Villa, Gaby Villa, Trish Sumida, and everyone around me who encouraged this work.

I am also grateful to Michael Ebeling and Kristina Holmes for bringing me to HCI Books, and Whitney Joiner for her contribution. A very special note of thanks goes to Candace Johnson, my editor, who had a vision for this book from day one and remained enthusiastic every step of the way. I am also very grateful to the whole team at HCI for their professionalism and positivity.

And to those who are unnamed but provided their stories, suggestions, and support while I was completing this book, I am most appreciative.

Resource Guide

The following is a list of resources that may enhance your understanding of confidence and happiness. Those previously mentioned in *Growing Happy Kids* are included (*see asterisks*):

Books

*Amen, Daniel, M.D. *Magnificent Mind at Any Age*, New York, NY: Harmony Books, 2008.

*Aron, Elaine. *The Highly Sensitive Child*. New York, NY: Three Rivers Press, 2002.

Brewer, Elizabeth Hartley. *Raising Confident Boys*. Cambridge, MA: Da Capo Press, 2001.

Davidson, Richard, and Sharon Begley. *The Emotional Life of Your Brain*. New York, NY: Hudson Street Press, 2012.

*Dweck, Carol. *Mindset: The New Psychology of Success*. New York, NY: Ballantine Books, 2007.

*Dyer, Wayne. *Incredible You*. Carlsbad, CA: Hay House, Inc., 2005.

Fox, Jennifer. *Your Child's Strengths*. New York, NY: Penguin Group, 2008.

*Frankl, Viktor. *Man's Search for Meaning*. New York, NY: Beacon Press, 2006, 1959

*Gelb, Michael J. *How to Think like Leonardo da Vinci*. New York, NY: Delta Trade Paperbacks, 2000.

*Ghandi, Mohandas K. *The Way to God*. Berkeley, CA: Berkeley Hills Books, 1999.

*Graimes, Nicola. *Brain Food for Kids*. London, England: Delta, 2005.

*Gyasto, Geshe Kelsang, trans. *Shantideva: A Guide to the Bodhisattva's Way of Life*. New York, NY: Tharpa Productions, 2002.

Hallowell, Edward, M.D. *The Childhood Roots of Adult Happiness*. New York, NY: Ballantine Books, 2002.

*Hay, Louise L. *The Power Is Within You*. Carlsbad, CA: Hay House, Inc., 1991.

Healy, Jane M. *Your Child's Growing Mind*. New York, NY: Broadway Books, 1987.

*Hicks, Jerry, and Esther Hicks. *Ask and It Is Given*. Carlsbad, CA: Hay House, Inc., 2005.

*His Holiness the Dalai Lama. *The Dalai Lama's Little Book of Wisdom*. Newburyport, MA: Hamptons Road Publishing, 2010.

———. *How to See Yourself As You Really Are*. New York, NY: Atria Books, 2006.

*———. *Live in a Better Way*. New York, NY: Penguin Compass, 1999.

*Kielburger, Craig, Marc Kielburger, and Shelley Page. *The World Needs Your Kid*. Berkeley, CA: Greystone Books, 2010.

McKenna, Ph.D., Paul. *I Can Make You Confident*. New York, NY: Sterling Publishing, 2010.

*Meade, Robin. *Morning Sunshine*. New York, NY: Center Street, 2009.

*Nhat Hanh, Thich. *The Art of Power*. New York, NY: HarperOne, 2007.

Ratey, John J. *A User's Guide to the Brain*. New York, NY: Vintage Books, 2001.

Richardson, Cheryl. *Stand Up for Your Life*. New York, NY: The Free Press, 2002.

Rinpoche, Yongey Mingyur. *The Joy of Living*. New York, NY: Three Rivers Press, 2007.

Salzberg, Sharon. *Real Happiness: The Power of Meditation*. New York, NY: Workman Publishing, 2010.

Sayre, Kent. *Unstoppable Confidence: How to Use the Power of NLP to Be More Dynamic and Successful*. New York, NY: McGraw Hill, 2008.

Schiraldi, Glenn. *10 Simple Solutions for Building Self-Esteem*. Oakland, CA: New Harbinger Publications, Inc., 2007.

Sharma, Robin. *The Monk Who Sold His Ferrari*. San Francisco, CA: HarperSanFrancisco, 1999.

Surya Das, Lama. *Awakening the Buddha Within*. New York, NY: Broadway Books, 1997.

*Virtue, Doreen. *Thank You, Angels*. Carlsbad, CA: Hay House, Inc., 2007.

*Wattles, Wallace. *The Science of Being Great*. Accessed at www.cslasheville.org/free_books.html/

*Wenig, Marsha. *Yoga Kids: Educating the Whole Child Through Yoga*. New York, NY: Stewart, Tabori, and Chang, 2003.

Music

*Hagan, Denise. "For Those Who Hear" from the album *For Those Who Hear*. Rosa Records, Sneezer Publishing: 2006. (www.denishagan.com)

*Jarry, Francine, and Abraham Hicks. "Joy, Joy, Joy" from the album *Joy, Joy, Joy*. Canada, Rainbow Music Company: 2006. (www.rainbowmusic.ca)

*Secret Agent 23 Skidoo. "Gotta Be Me" from the album *Easy*. Underground Playground, 2008. (secretagent23skidoo.com)

Audio

*Peale, Norman Vincent. *The Power of Positive Thinking*. New York, NY: Simon & Schuster Audio, 1992.

Canfield, Jack. *Maximum Confidence: 10 Secrets of Extreme Self-Esteem*. New York, NY: Simon & Schuster Radio, 1989.

*Chodron, Pema. *Unconditional Confidence*. Louisville, CO: Sounds True, 2010.

Video

A&E Biography. *Dalai Lama—The Soul of Tibet*. New York, NY: New Video, 1997.

*McNamara, Sean, Deborah Schwartz, et al. *Soul Surfer*. Hollywood, CA: Film District and Tristar Pictures, 2011.

*Simunye, Thina. *We Are Together*. New York, NY: Palm Pictures, 2006.

Internet

*Bruce Perry from ChildTrauma Academy, accessed in August 2011.

*Denis Waitley quote accessed on January 28, 2011.

Late Late Show with Craig Ferguson and Simon Helberg on May 16, 2011.

Late Late Show with Craig Ferguson and Condoleezza Rice on Oct. 25, 2010.

*Nemours quote accessed on March 1, 2011 from the Nemours Foundation website at www.nemours.org.

*Pema Chodron quote, accessed on March 1, 2011.

Richard Davidson on neuroscience, www.being.publicradio.org/programs/2011/healthy-minds, accessed November, 2011

*Rumi quote accessed on March 1, 2011.

*Science Daily, accessed January 28, 2011 http://www.sciencedaily.com/releases/2009/01/090108082904.htm.

*Thich Nhat Hanh quote, accessed on January 28, 2011.

Index

A
abuse
  brain development and, 58
  inner confidence and, 190–92
academics, as potential problem, 167
acknowledgement, important role of,
  175
activities
  as affirming, 120
  brain development and, 57
  happiness and, 151
adversity
  happiness and, 144–45
  myth of, 27
  refugee experience and, 36–37
  resilience to (*see* resilience)
affection
  brain development and, 57
  important role of, 98, 103
affirmations
  adversity and, 146–47
  for confidence, 117
  confidence feedback loops and, 79,
    80
  exercise for confidence, 103–4
  important role of, 207, 215–17
  inner feedback and, 83–84
  parents and, 110–12

specific examples of, 216
alcohol, brain development and, 57
Alcoholics Anonymous, 88
allemansrätten, 44
altruism. *See* caring; compassion
Amen, Daniel, 56, 57
amygdala, brain development and, 60
analytical intelligence, 83
analytical meditation, 217–18
anger, inner confidence and, 21
anxiety
  chemical imbalance and, 57
  mindfulness and, 228
Aron, Elaine, 192
Art of Power, The (Hanh), 111
arts
  important role of, 229–30
  spirituality and, 127
Ask and It Is Given (Hicks & Hicks), 116
athletics, 99–100. *See also* exercise
atmosphere, confidence feedback
    loops and, 80–81
audio assistance, 230
Aurelius, Marcus, 215
authenticity, inner confidence and, 82
awareness, Emotional Scale of
    Confidence and, 71

B
Barton, Bruce, 13
Battle Hymn of the Tiger Mother
    (Chua), 29
Beckwith, Michael Bernard, 202
bedtime, 100–101. *See also* sleep
behavior problems, brain
    development and, 58
beliefs
    breaks to, 170
    as building block, 61–67, 90, 91*f*,
        206
    in children, 111
    false, 185 (*see also* false beliefs)
    implementing changes for, 105–12
    skillful, 185 (*see also* skillful beliefs)
belonging. *See* community
Big Bang Theory, The, 105
biology
    breaks to, 169
    as building block, 56–59, 90, 91*f*, 206
    implementing changes for, 98–104
blocks. *See* Five Building Blocks of
    Confidence
brain development, 56–59, 101
Brain Food for Kids (Graimes), 102
breathing techniques, "Hot Soup
    Breath", 147–48
Buddhist teaching, 199
    "Buddha seed" and, 74, 89
    confidence and, 138
    ethics of, 197–202
    happiness and, 136–38
health and, 225
meditation and, 217–18
"A Precious Human Life"
    (Dalai Lama), 212
building blocks. *See* Five Building
    Blocks of Confidence
bullying, 34, 167, 172–74

C
caffeine, brain development and, 57

calmness, happiness and, 147–50
Campbell, Joseph, 14, 30
car rides, as opportunity for
    sharing, 210
caring
    cultivating, 199–201
    happiness and, 142–44, 151
causality, law of, 198
certainty in tasks, Emotional Scale
    of Confidence and, 71
chakras, 225
challenges. *See* adversity
charity, 151, 230–31. *See also*
    compassion
chemical imbalances, brain
    development and, 57
Child Fund International, 231
children
    depression and, 196
    developing confidence in, 14–15
    exceptional, 195–96
    highly sensitive, 192–94
    people pleasers, 196
    perfectionists, 196
    stages of confidence in, 24–26
    wounded, 190–92
ChildTrauma Academy, 190
Chodron, Pema, 115, 145
Chopra, Deepak, 85–86
Christian prayer, "Good Morning,
    God" (Healy), 213
Chua, Amy, 29
Coleman, Ben, 87
community. *See also* support
    important role of, 40–42, 46–47, 207
compassion
    Eastern tradition and, 199–201
    happiness and, 151
    inner confidence and, 21
competitions, confidence feedback
    loops and, 120
confidence
    anchoring, 106–7

breaking of, 158–59
children's stages of, 24–26
corrections to, 168–69
direction toward, 63–64
feedback loops and (*see* confidence
    feedback loops)
happiness and, 138–39, 140–41
    (*see also* happiness)
inner (*see* inner confidence)
myths of, 26–27
outer (*see* outer confidence)
over-, 27
as revolution, 232–33
science of, 59–61
vs. self-esteem, 18–19
signs of problems with, 162–66
stages of, 22–24
confidence feedback loops, 76–79, 78*f*
    important role of, 175
    inner, 82–85, 121
    outer, 79–82
    social skill development and,
        120–23
consciousness, 85–86
core-strength movement, confidence
    feedback loops and, 79
counseling, wounded children and,
    191–92
courage, confidence and, 16
creative expression. *See also* arts
    evaluation of, 85
    important role of, 229–30
Creative Visions Foundation, 75–76
criticism
    highly sensitive children and, 194
    as potential problem, 167
culture
    bullying and, 34
    family as, 39
    inner confidence and, 48–49
    parenting differences and, 30
    refugee experience and, 36–38

D
Dalai Lama (His Holiness the
    Fourteenth), 21, 131, 142, 197,
    211
Davidson, Richard, 59, 60
depression
    brain development and, 58
    chemical imbalance and, 57
    mindfulness and, 228
    as special consideration, 196
disability. *See also* exceptional children
    as potential problem, 167
doubt
    of children, 111
    mindfulness and, 228
    as problem, 174–75
    of self (*see* self-doubt)
dream journals, 124–25
Dweck, Carol, 175
Dyer, Wayne, 107, 160, 209

E
earth awareness, importance of, 44–45
Eastern tradition, 197. *See also*
    Buddhist teaching
eating habits. *See* nutrition
Eldon, Kathy, 75–76
Emotional Scale of Confidence, 68, 71
emotions
    brain development and, 60
    breaks to, 170
    as building block, 67–75, 90, 91*f*,
        206–7
    implementing changes for, 112–19
empathy, inner confidence and, 82
empowerment
    daily, 209–10
    ideas and, 209
    sources of, 210–11
environment
    brain development and, 57
    highly sensitive children and, 194
    important role of, 207

ethics, Eastern tradition and, 197–202
etiquette, important role of, 45–46
evaluation. *See also* feedback of life, 85
exceptional children, 195–96
exercise
  for biology, 103–5
  brain development and, 57
  breathing, 147–48
  for confidence, 116–18, 211
  as confidence feedback loop, 121
  for happiness, 151
  important role of, 98–100, 206,
    225–27
  meditation, 220–21 (*see also*
    meditation)
  for social skills, 122–23, 123–25
  for spirituality, 128–29
  spirituality and, 127
existential intelligence, 83
expectations, as potential problem, 165
experiences
  confidence and, 95
  confidence feedback loops and,
    79–80
  as potential problem, 166–67
  wisdom and, 96–97
external influences on confidence.
    See outer confidence

F
failure, mindfulness and, 228
faith, Emotional Scale of Confidence
    and, 68, 71
false beliefs, inner confidence and,
    185, 186
family, important role of, 39–40
fear, Emotional Scale of Confidence
    and, 68, 71
feedback. *See also* confidence
    feedback loops
  confidence feedback loops, 78*f*
  inner, 77
  inner confidence and, 38

  outer, 77
feelings. *See also* confidence feedback
    loops, inner; emotions
  of confidence, 112–14
  important role of, 206, 207
  inner vs. outer confidence and, 115
Field, Sally, 73
Fillmore, Charles, 72
fish oil, brain development and, 57
Five Building Blocks of Confidence
  basics of, 55–56, 206–7
  beliefs, 61–67, 105–12, 206
  biology, 56–59, 98–104, 206
  breaks to, 169–71
  connecting, 89–91, 91*f*
  corrections to, 168
  development of, 55
  emotions, 67–75, 112–19, 206–7
  as framework, 202–3
  as model, 54
  social, 75–85
  social skills, 119–26, 207
  spiritual, 85–89, 126–29, 207
  strength building and, 197
  synergistic nature of, 129–30
fleeting happiness. *See* happiness
food. *See* nutrition
"For Those Who Hear" (Hagan), 209
Ford, Harrison, 150
Frankl, Victor, 72
freedom for exploration.
    See independence
Freud. Anna, 151–57
friendships. *See also* role models as
    potential problem, 164, 167

G
Gandhi, Mohandas, 181
Gelb, Michael J., 79
gifted children. *See* exceptional
    children
Goddard, Anne, 31–33
Goddard, Colin, 31–33

Golden Rule, 198
"Good Morning, God" (Healy), 213
Goodall, Jane, 202
"Gotta Be Me" (Secret Agent 23 Skidoo), 223–24
Gottman, John, 67
grades, confidence feedback loops and, 79–80, 120
Graimes, Nicola, 102
greatness, 107
group mindset. *See* community
growth, adversity and, 36–37
Guide to the Bodhisattva's Way of Life, A (Shantideva), 106

H
Habitat for Humanity, 231
Hagan, Denise, 209, 221
Hamilton, Bethany, 143
Hanh, Thich Nhat, 111, 136, 227
Hanuman, 34
happiness
    calmness and, 147–50
    caring for others and, 142–44
    challenges and, 144–45
    confidence and, 138–39, 140–41
    developing as practice, 150–52
    fleeting vs. lasting, 132–34, 151–52
    "how to", 134–36
    inner confidence and, 15, 54
    key messages of, 151–52
    meaning and, 87
hatred, of self. *See* self-hatred
Hay, Louise, 107, 209
health, evaluation of, 85
Healy, Maureen, 213
Helberg, Simon, 105
hesitancy, as potential problem, 163
Hicks, Esther, 116, 202
Hicks, Jerry, 116
Highly Sensitive Child, The (Aron), 192
highly sensitive children, 192–94
Holder, Mark, 87

Holmes, Ernest, 96–97, 107
honesty, 197–98
"Hot Soup Breath", 147–48
How to Think Like Leonardo da Vinci (Gelb), 79
human life, potential of, 106
hydration
    brain development and, 57
    important role of, 98, 102–3

I
"I Am Everything" (Hagan), 209
Ibsen, Henrik, 174
ideas, connection to, 209
identity, confidence and, 17–18
immigration, stories of, 36–38
Incredible You! (Dyer), 107, 209
independence
    important role of, 43–45
    inner confidence and, 31–33
inner confidence. *See also* confidence
    art of, 38
    building blocks of (*see* Five Building Blocks of Confidence)
    characteristics of, 24
    cross cultural nature of, 48–49
    cultivating with outer confidence, 177–78
    dynamic nature of, 231–32
    Emotional Scale of Confidence and, 71
    feelings of, 115
    happiness and, 15, 54, 151–52 (*see also* happiness)
    independence and, 31–33
    lifetime impact of, 203
    misperceptions and, 187–88
    modeling of, 28
    path to, 178–79
    as path to true power, 20–22
    personality considerations and, 190–96
    spirituality and, 31–33

inner confidence. *See also* confidence
    (cont'd from page 247)
  as stage, 23, 25
  three-step process for, 181–85
  transition to, 114–16
inner feedback, 77
inner power, 62–63
inner praise, 176
insecurity, Emotional Scale of
    Confidence and, 71
inspiration, highly sensitive children
    and, 194
instincts, confidence and, 16
intelligence
  emotional (*see* emotions)
  exceptional children and, 195–96
  multiple, 83
interfaith prayer, "Today" (Healy), 213
interpersonal feedback. *See* outer
    feedback
intrapersonal feedback. *See* inner
    feedback
intuition, confidence and, 16

J
Jarry, Francine, 223
Jeremy Fisher (Potter), 112
Johnson, Lady Bird, 195
journaling, 124–25
"Joy, Joy, Joy" (Jarry), 223
juices. *See* hydration
Jung, Carl, 68, 144, 191

K
karate, 226. *See also* exercise
Karate Kid, The, 104
karma, 198
Keilburger, Craig, 199
Keilburger, Marc, 199

L
Laboratory for Affective Neuroscience,
    59

Lao Tzu, 201
Larson, Christian D., 177
lasting happiness. *See* happiness
Late Late Show with Craig Ferguson,
    104
law of causality, 198
learning activities, brain development
    and, 57
Lembo, John, 82
life, potential of, 106
Lincoln, Abraham, 134
linguistic intelligence, 83

M
Magnificent Mind at Any Age
    (Amen), 56
Man's Search for Meaning
    (Frankl), 72
Marino, Dan, 93
material considerations, spirituality
    and, 34–35
Meade, Robin, 115
meal time. *See also* nutrition
  important role of, 39–40
  inner confidence and, 37–38
meaning, happiness and, 87
measurements, confidence feedback
    loops and, 79–80
meditation. *See also* mindfulness
  brain development and, 58
  as confidence feedback loop, 121
  happiness and, 151
  important role of, 48, 217–21
  inner confidence and (*see also*
    spirituality)
  inner feedback and, 83–84
  loving-kindness, 128–29
  walking, 149–50
Michelangelo, 178
Milne, A.A., 112
mind movies, 230
mindfulness. *See also* meditation
  as confidence feedback loop, 121

Emotional Scale of Confidence and,
71
important role of, 227–29
mirror exercises, confidence feedback
loops and, 79
misperceptions
identification of, 187–88
inner confidence and, 185–86
modeling. *See* role models
Monk Who Sold His Ferrari, The
(Sharma), 63
Morning Sunshine (Meade), 115
Motivate2Learn, 162
movement. *See also* exercise
confidence feedback loops and, 79
important role of, 207, 225–27
intelligence, 83
spirituality and, 127
multivitamins, brain development
and, 57
music
as confidence feedback loop, 121
important role of, 221–25
specific examples of, 222–24
spirituality and, 127
musical intelligence, 83
Myss, Caroline, 14, 209, 234

N
nature
importance of, 44–45
meditation and, 150
spirituality and, 127
negative thinking. *See* pessimism
Nemours Health & Prevention Services,
75
*New Psychology of Success,
The* (Dweck), 175
nondemoninational prayer, "Prayer for
Peace" (Gandhi), 214
nutrition, 101–2
brain development and, 57
highly sensitive children and, 194

important role of, 98, 206

O
omega-3 fatty acids, brain development
and, 57
opportunity, important role of, 175
optimism
brain development and, 58
Emotional Scale of Confidence
and, 71
experiences and, 98
important role of, 108–9
outer confidence
breaking of, 160–61
challenges of, 28
characteristics of, 23–24
cultivating with inner confidence,
177–78
described, 16–18
Emotional Scale of Confidence
and, 71
feelings of, 115
misperceptions and, 187–88
as stage, 22, 25
transitioning from, 114–16
outer feedback, 77, 78*f*, 79–82

P
parents
development of beliefs and, 65–66
words of, 110–12
parkour, 226. *See also* exercise
"Peace Corners", 148–49
Peale, Norman Vincent, 61, 205
peer support. *See* support
people pleasers, 196
perception, culture and, 30
"Perfect Replications" (Hagan), 221
perfectionists, 196
Perry, Bruce, 190
Peter Rabbit (Potter), 112
physical signs, as potential problem,
165–66, 167

Picasso, Pablo, 65
"Pizza Slice" game, 118
placement meditation, 217–18
"Positive Things" game, 117–18
positive thinking. *See* optimism
posture, as potential problem, 165–66
potential
    of human life, 106
    inner confidence and, 21
    spirituality and, 85–86
Potter, Beatrix, 112
power
    experiences and, 97
    . inner, 62–63, 107
Power Is Within You, The (Hay), 107
Power of Positive Thinking, The (Peale),
    61
praise. *See also* feedback
    highly sensitive children and, 194
    important role of, 175–77
    inner confidence and, 82
prayer
    confidence feedback loops and, 79,
        96
    "Good Morning, God" (Healy), 213
    important role of, 48, 211–12
    inner confidence and (*see also*
        spirituality)
    "Prayer for Peace" (Gandhi), 214
    "A Precious Human Life" (Dalai
        Lama), 212
    spirituality and, 127
    "Today" (Healy), 213
"Prayer for Peace" (Gandhi), 214
"Precious Human Life, A" (Dalai Lama),
    212
prefrontal cortex, brain development
    and, 60
pregnancy, brain development and, 57

Q
quality time, important role of, 42–43

R
refugee experience, stories of, 36–38
rejection, mindfulness and, 228
relationships, evaluation of, 85
reliance, self-. *See* self-reliance
religion, 87. *See also* spirituality
reluctance, as potential problem, 163
repetition, confidence feedback loops
    and, 79–80
resilience, inner confidence and, 20–21
Rice, Condoleezza, 65–66
risk taking, inner confidence and, 21
ritual. *See* routine; spirituality
Robbins, Tony, 62–63
role models
    breaking confidence and, 158
    confidence feedback loops and, 81
    empowerment and, 210–11
    happiness and, 151
    highly sensitive children and, 194
    of inner confidence, 28
routine
    as affirming, 120
    bedtime, 100–101
    important role of, 39–40, 206
    inner confidence and, 37–38
    stories as part of, 112
Rumi, 27

S
Sacred Contracts (Myss), 234
sadness. *See* depression
safety, children and, 65
schedule. *See* routine
school, as potential problem, 167
Science Daily, 87
Science of Being Great, The (Wattles),
    84, 86, 107
Science of Mind, 96–97, 107
Sears, William, 103
secondhand smoke, brain
    development and, 57
Secret, The (Waitley), 215

Secret Agent 23 Skidoo, 223–24
security
    children and, 65
    Emotional Scale of Confidence
        and, 71
self, sense of. *See* inner confidence
self-assuredness, Emotional Scale of
        Confidence and, 71
self-confidence. *See* confidence
self-doubt. *See also* beliefs; uncertainty
    chemical imbalance and, 57
    Emotional Scale of Confidence and,
        71
    inner confidence and, 20
    myth of, 26–27
self-esteem, 18–19
self-hatred, inner confidence and, 20
self-love, Emotional Scale of
        Confidence and, 71
self-reliance, 33
self-talk. *See also* affirmations;
        confidence feedback loops, inner
negative, 159
self-talk, negative, 164–65
self-trust
    Emotional Scale of Confidence
        and, 71
    inner confidence and, 33
sensitive children, 192–94
Seven Spiritual Laws of Success,
    The (Chopra), 85–86
sexual activity, brain development
    and, 58
Shakespeare, William, 110
Shantideva, 106
Sharma, Robin, 63
Sivananda, Swami, 147
skillful beliefs, inner confidence and,
    185, 186–87
skills, as potential problem, 167
sleep
    brain development and, 57
    important role of, 98, 100–101, 206

slouching, as potential problem,
    165–66
smoking, brain development and, 57
social skills
    breaks to, 170–71
    as building block, 75–85, 91, 91*f*,
        207
    implementing changes for, 119–26
    important role of, 45–46
solitude, as potential problem, 163–64
songs, confidence feedback loops and,
    79
Soul Surfer, 143
spiritual mind treatments. *See* prayer
spirituality. *See also* meditation; prayer
    belonging and, 40–42
    breaks to, 171
    as building block, 85–89, 91, 91*f*,
        126–29, 207
    as confidence feedback loop, 121
    important role of, 47–48
    inner confidence and, 31–33
strength
    inner confidence and, 21
    special circumstances and, 196–97
stress, mindfulness and, 228
success, visualization of, 111
support. *See also* community
    brain development and, 58
    highly sensitive children and, 194
    important role of, 207
    social skills and, 76

T
tai chi chuan, 226. *See also* exercise
talent, confidence as, 26
television, brain development and, 57
Teresa of Avila (Saint), 89
Thank You, Angels! (Virtue), 209
third-culture childhood, inner
        confidence and, 31–33

thoughts
    emotions and, 68, 72–73
    important role of, 206
time together, important role of, 42–43
"Today" (Healy), 213
toxins, brain development and, 57
trauma, inner confidence and, 190–92
trust
    breaking confidence and, 158
    inner confidence and, 82
    self- (*see* self-trust)
Tzu, Lao, 201

U
uncertainty. *See also* self-doubt
    characteristics of, 23
    chemical imbalance and, 57
    Emotional Scale of Confidence
        and, 71
    as stage, 22, 25
Unconditional Confidence
        (Chodron), 115

V
verbal feedback, 79–80
Virginia Tech shooting, 31–33
Virtue, Doreen, 209
visualization

meditation, 218–20
    of success, 111
vitamins, brain development and, 57

W
Waitley, Denis, 215
walking meditation, 149–50
Wallace, Judi, 87
water. *See* hydration
Wattles, Wallace, 84, 86, 107
wealth, evaluation of, 85
Weihenmayer, Erik, 62
Winfrey, Oprah, 183
Winnie the Pooh (Milne), 112
wisdom
    Eastern tradition and, 201–2
    experiences and, 96–97
    important role of, 206
words. *See* affirmations
World Needs Your Kid, The (Keilburger
        & Keilburger), 199
worry. *See* anxiety
wounded children, 190–92, 196
Wright, Robin, 53

Y
yoga, 226. *See also* exercise